31 DAYS TO
FINDING YOUR
Inner
Sass

31 Days to Finding Your Inner Sass:
Shortcuts to Girlfriend Happiness

Copyright ©2012 by Shari Goldsmith

ISBN-13: 978-1-57074-018-3

Printed in the United States of America

Cover Design and Printing By:

Greyden Press, LLC
2251 Arbor Blvd.
Dayton, OH 45439
www.greydenpress.com

Contents

Are you Ready to Find Your Inner Sass?

It happens to me all the time. At one event or another, a girlfriend will come up to me and announce, "I certainly don't need any help finding *my* inner sass. In fact, I have too much sass." Really? I'm not so sure about that. See, inner sass doesn't mean you yell louder than anyone else in the room. It certainly doesn't mean you know how to tell people off. Let me explain from the beginning.

I was married at the young age of twenty-two. I met my would-be husband during my first year of college, actually on the first day of school! I certainly didn't know at that moment that I would end up marrying him, even though he claims he immediately knew. What I did know is that I really enjoyed being around him and that I wanted to spend more time with him. From the first time I met him, I sensed that he was a great, interesting person AND he was good for me.

Looking back now, twenty-two seems awfully young, don't you think? How could I have possibly known what I wanted? Yet, we're still happily married and just celebrated our thirtieth wedding anniversary. Now don't get me wrong: Marriage has not always been easy, and life has not always been fabulous. Frankly, there have been both good times and bad. But I believe the reason for our success has been that the good **definitely** outweighs the bad.

During our marriage, there have been times when we've had to scrape money together for a McMeal, while at other times, we've had the freedom to do and buy whatever we pleased. We've had horrible arguments that lasted late into the night; yes, we've kept right on fighting until **he** invariably fell asleep and left me angry and unable to sleep a wink. We've also had times when we've gotten along wonderfully and felt incredibly lucky to be together. The most important thing is that I can't even remember what we were fighting about! I suppose that means that WHAT we were fighting about probably was not earth shattering.

As our marriage progressed, we weathered losing all four of our parents. We had to watch the slow, painful process as our beloved parents' health began to fail and they lost their will to live. Those were times of great stress and pain, and we really needed the support of each other to make it through.

During our thirty years together, we raised two incredible sons who have turned into great young men. No, I didn't say my kids are perfect; I said they are *great* young men. They are really good people with a whole lot of character. They are kind, perceptive, strong, and independent and have a good sense of who they are. Yes, they made their fair share of mistakes while growing up. Yes, I remember the police calling to say they had my younger son in custody and I needed to pick him up. Let's just say it wasn't his best moment, but thanks to my inner sass, maybe it was mine. While my sons were growing up, we enjoyed times of great joy and fun, but we also had to endure many horrific fights. There were times when our two boys were at each other's throats and times when they professed their love and support for one another. There were times when I was ready to quit the motherhood thing altogether and times when I realized it was my finest role in life.

Just like motherhood and marriage, I've had good times and bad times in my career. I've been lucky enough to work in many different fields with a vast array of experiences throughout my career. When I first graduated from college with a degree in communications, there were very few jobs available—not that I had any inkling what I wanted to do in life because I was only twenty-two years old. How do you really know what you want at that age? I was lucky to be selected for a job as an assistant manager in retail. That plum position paid me the large sum of $12,000 a year!

I soon realized that my skills and talents were a good fit

for the retailing field. As the company grew from two store operations to fifty, I grew with them. I quickly moved up to co-manager, manager, and eventually district manager. Thanks to my high energy level, I jumped at the opportunity to create many of the systems and programs utilized within the company. I developed their training program and their merchandising guidelines and was their troubleshooter for addressing store operations that were not profitable. I realized I had a talent for recognizing what was missing in an organization and developing a plan to implement the process change.

After a while, though, I finally reached the point where the position had run its course. I took a job in outside sales that allowed me to travel all over the state, selling eyewear to optometrists. Although it was not a good fit for me, it afforded me with invaluable skills that I could add to my repertoire for future positions.

In my next job, I was able to put my creativity to good use. By that time, I knew where I excelled: developing new processes and programs. I worked in the schools and developed a variety of programs to connect school curriculum with real-world experience. I developed vital business partnerships for the schools and created and presented numerous workshops and programs.

After that position ran its course, I was asked to head up a committee tasked with bringing a team together to develop case plans for emotionally disturbed children. I stepped into that role with limited experience in the field. During my stay there, I created a program that met the needs for those children in their own community. I changed the way the government system worked, even when everyone said it wasn't possible, and the program was so successful that it eventually grew from three employees to thirty.

At that point in life, I made a decision. I had always wanted to return to school to become a mental health therapist but was hesitant to take the plunge. Going to school was out of my comfort zone, but that was exactly why I decided to do it. Then, after working in the nonprofit field as a mental health therapist, I decided my skills would be best utilized if I combined all my experience and became a women's life coach...and the rest is history.

So why am I sharing *my* whole story when I'm supposed to be talking about finding *your* inner sass? As I look back, I now realize that every successful accomplishment and experience I've experienced in my life was due to the fact that I have my inner sass. That doesn't mean I haven't made my fair share—and maybe then some—of mistakes in my personal and professional life. What it does mean is that I've lived my life by following certain principles. These principles have enabled me to accomplish my defined goals and have supported me during the times when I've failed to meet my own and others' expectations. These guidelines have enabled me to nurture a great long-term relationship, while supporting me when things have gotten tough. These rules in life have enabled me to be an excellent mother and raise happy, healthy kids, and they have gotten me through the rough times when things seemed pretty bleak. The bottom line is that this life perspective has guided me to be happy and healthy, and it has gotten me to where I am today.

Do you feel like you have your inner sass most of the time? Good for you, but even women who have plenty of inner sass need a little maintenance now and then. At times, each one of us veers off course, and we need a tune-up to get back on track. We need to take some time out to reevaluate our personal and professional lives and be reminded of the principles that help us stay healthy and happy.

My hope for you, girlfriend, is that you will take the time to read through the 31 days to finding your inner sass and do some thinking about your own life. At the end of each section, you will find "Give It a Little More Thought" questions, which will help you give some thought as to how each chapter actually relates to your own life. The questions will enable you to delve a little deeper into each topic. You will also find "Your Call to Action" exercises that will give you the opportunity to further engage on that specific topic.

Be sure to revisit each section now and any time when you are struggling with a specific principle in your life.

Girlfriends, don't wait another day to change your life. Find your inner sass!

Knock! Knock! "Who's There?"

A couple months ago, I attended a workshop on discovering your strengths in life. The speaker began the discussion by asking the women in the room to write down the strengths they felt they possessed. I quickly filled out my sheet and finished the task. When I looked up from my work and around the room, I was shocked to see that the majority of women were struggling to write ANYTHING down on paper. They were just frozen with their pens in their hand, as if they couldn't find a single strength within them.

Try it! Make a list of your Top 3 Strengths

1.

2.

3.

I believe that what made it such a difficult task was that as women, we often see ourselves limited to the roles we play. We are someone's daughter, mother, wife, coach, granddaughter, or employee. Over time, those roles and responsibilities slowly become our whole identity, and we become confused as to who we really are "down deep at the core." Disconnected with that unique person we were meant to be, we become dissatisfied with our lives. We know life can certainly have more purpose and passion, but we are at a loss as how to find it and where the heck to start looking.

Be honest: I'm sure you can name a couple of times in your life (in all probability, more than that) when you have had to deny your needs for the needs of a boyfriend, husband, child, friend, boss, or someone else. I know I have. We put ourselves last on the list because we tend to be givers, often to the extreme of self-sacrifice. Over time, we lose sight of our best self and what we really need in order to be happy.

Sometimes, we actually deny ourselves in exchange for becoming what others want us to be. Perhaps this stems from a learned pattern in our childhood, one we repeat time and time again in each of our various relationships because it is what feels familiar and comfortable. After a while, the thought of trying to figure out who we are becomes scary and overwhelming, so we rationalize and try to convince ourselves that things are just fine, even when they aren't. Do you know what we call this behavior? **Settling!**

So, how do you start finding your true self? What is the first step toward finding or rediscovering your sass? Just begin by making a list of the qualities, values, and strengths you possess now—at *this* very moment in your life. Remember not to list your roles or responsibilities, *just* your strengths. Once you have that list, make a list of the qualities, values, strengths, and goals you aspire to possess in life. After you've got both of your lists as complete as you can get them, take a good look at them for the sake of comparison. Do they closely align with one another, or are they very different? Obviously, the closer these align, the closer you are to living true to yourself, to the real you!

Now, DON'T PANIC if you're having trouble making either of your lists, as this happens a lot in the beginning of the journey. Maybe it would help you to think back to when you were a little girl or a teenager. What did you enjoy doing then? Did you create art projects or love running around and playing outside? Did you love cooking, sewing, sports, or music? Were you obsessed with reading, or did you have a knack for writing? Give this some thought.

After you have made your list, I want you to think about your life for a moment. Do you live your life with passion and energy? Here's the real truth: The more you live "true to you" and your talents, the more energy, confidence, and exuberance you will have in life. If you are not living your life honestly and "true to you," it will feel as though you're swimming upstream, constantly fighting the current. Your days will literally drain you of energy.

Do you speak to what you truly feel, or do you constantly hear yourself speaking to please others? Are you using your signature strengths and gifts **daily**? Now, here's the kicker: Are you living your life by the values and goals you have always aspired to obtain?

This is not easy work, girlfriends! This rollercoaster ride can be scary and challenging, and it often entails taking risks and embracing change, but if you have the courage to change, good things will come your way. At the end of your journey, you will find a life filled with contentment, passion, and genuine happiness.

Congratulations! You are on the road to finding your inner sass!

"Change only occurs when YOU are ready for it."

Give it a Little More Thought, Girlfriend

visit 3 1. What strengths, if any, do you utilize on a daily basis?

_____

_____

_____

_____

_____

_____

2. Be honest: Are you presently living true to who you really are? Why or why not?

_____

_____

_____

_____

_____

_____

Your Call to Action

For seven days, keep a log of the individual strengths you use throughout each day. After a week, take a look at your log. Are you using your signature strengths on a consistent basis? What changes can you make to your life that will enable you to utilize more of your skills and talents?

_____

_____

_____

_____

_____

_____

Gee...Why do Bad Things Have to Happen?

There is no way to make it through life without having your share—or sometimes more than your fair share—of disappointments. Life is **NOT** made up of just one good time after another! Eventually and inevitably, we all get smacked in the face with something painful. Let's face it, life can be a rollercoaster of emotional ups and downs—good times followed by bad times followed by good times. But here's the reality: When times are good, we don't do a lot of growing and changing. We might enjoy the time and feel on top of the world, but we don't really come to any better understanding of our lives and where we belong; instead, we just revel in the ride until things get bad again. Not everyone uses these "bad" times to grow as an individual. Some girlfriends have difficulty moving through the phases that are needed in order for them to accept their new reality. Now, be honest with yourself and think back to the last bad curve life threw at you. Which category did you fall into?

When I was a mental health therapist, I worked with individuals who struggled with the realities of cancer. Some were able to live long, productive lives, while others could not. A few of my clients knew their lives were nearing an end and that their days were numbered. I remember asking them on one occasion if they felt that the cancer was a gift. This angered one individual, and he stated that if it was, indeed, a gift, he wanted to return it with the receipt! I can't say I blamed him. Two other individuals replied that their lives were "far richer" and "more rewarding" than they were before they received their cancer diagnosis. Richer and rewarding because of cancer? Does that surprise you?

The reality is this: Bad things are going to happen now and then. Our lack of control over our lives is a big factor in our unhappiness. But, like the clients living with cancer, we have a choice of how we want to deal and cope with the accompanied feelings that come with any supposed downturn of events. Do our lives become clearer to us in those grim moments? Do we better understand who we are and what we need to be happy? Do we begin to understand whom we want to allow into our lives? Do we search for meaning and purpose, or do we spiral down in anger over life's unfairness and uncertainty? Now don't get me wrong: The feelings of shock and anger are all part of the process of recovery, completely normal. One MUST go through these changes to get to the other side. The problem is, though, that many individuals get "stuck in the muck" and end up drowning there.

They never, ever, ever leave...

I network with diverse groups of women in my daily work. A while back, I had plans to meet an attorney at her office and then go out to lunch with her. When I arrived, the secretary informed me that my friend was running a little late with a client, so I sat down and grabbed a magazine to relax. As I began to read, I heard loud sounds emanating from my friend's office. Soon, the screaming and crying was loud enough for me to make out every word being said. I could tell a divorce case was the cause of the commotion, and the woman was angry and hurt. Considering that emotions often run high during the divorce process, it really didn't come as much of a surprise. By the time the woman finally left twenty minutes later, my friend looked exhausted and spent. As we headed out for lunch, I commented, "Wow! That must be one horrific divorce case." She turned to me and said, "You don't understand. It has been eight years since her divorce, but she just won't let go and move on."

This is a perfect example of a woman who experienced a bad turn in her life and has had difficulty moving beyond the experience. Instead of building a new life and reinventing herself, she is stuck in the muck and refuses to get out. She has wasted *EIGHT YEARS* being miserable. She has wasted *EIGHT YEARS* when she could be enjoying life and building a new community for herself. But instead, she keeps replaying the hurt and anger from the past.

An important part of finding your inner sass is learning how to navigate such bad times. The keys to moving forward during such a phase are to give yourself permission to feel and continue to trudge through it. It's about being honest in your emotions and pushing yourself forward to understand "you" better. It is about accepting what life throws at you, no matter how difficult that may be. Last, it's about taking it one day at a time until things get a little better.. And they will! **I promise!**

All girlfriends have problems. Some of us face our problems head on, deal and rise above them. Others allow our problems to consume us and color our lives negatively. Every girlfriend has a choice. Remember that.

Give it a Little More Thought, Girlfriend

1. Think about a difficult time in your life. How did you change as a person, positive or negative, as a result of that experience?

_____

_____

_____

_____

_____

_____

2. If you were to go through that same experience today, would you have the same reaction? If not, how would it be different?

_____

_____

_____

_____

_____

_____

Your Call To Action

Make a list of the positive coping skills you can use when life gets difficult. At the same time, make a list of the negative coping skills you have used in the past. Which positive coping skills on your list can you use the next time you are feeling vulnerable?

_____

_____

_____

_____

_____

_____

Girlfriend Cliff's Notes for a Great Relationship

Do you know the essentials to a great relationship? If not, would you like to? Follow along while I list the ingredients needed for relationship success!

You have your own interests, goals, and identity. You know who you are, independent of your significant other, and you know what you want in life.

I meet girlfriends daily who have absolutely no sense of who they are. It is as if they are searching for someone to help them decide who they are and what they like. Don't fall into this pattern! If you are in a relationship and you aren't clear about who you are, that relationship will struggle to survive. It might work for you at first, but somewhere down the line, you will become dissatisfied and lost! The chances of you being happy and successful in such a relationship are slim to none. How can you be happy unless you know what you are looking for? How can you know what you are looking for unless you understand yourself better and understand what you need? See what I mean? I beg of you: Do the work before you fall into a relationship. A healthy relationship is made up of two people who know what they stand for and what they need to be happy in life.

You have a similar set of values and goals in life.

When it comes to the most important things in life, you pretty much agree. That doesn't mean a Democrat can't marry a Republican. It has been done and can work quite well! It just means that on the majority of issues like religion, standards and styles of living, or your vision of the future, the two of you agree or can come to a happy medium. If you practice different religions and neither will compromise whatsoever, it might be an issue when children arrive. If one of you wants children and the other does not, that is a major sticking point for a successful relationship. Remember that you can't count on your partner to change; you must assume that the person you know at this moment is the one you will be with forever. Are you willing to accept that?

The two of you are able to communicate your needs and concerns to each other in an emotionally healthy manner.

This doesn't mean it's wrong to fight every now and then. Come on! You're both individuals with your own opinions, needs, expectations, and so on. What I *am* saying is that you both fight fairly without using manipulation tactics or exhibiting passive-aggressive behavior. If you don't feel comfortable discussing issues with your partner because he won't understand, that is a huge red flag! In a healthy relationship, you are both able to articulate what you need to be happy in life. If this is difficult for you, you need to further define exactly what you need in life to be happy.

The two of you are very good friends.

Do you know what this statement should mean to you? You should trust and respect each other and know that you can count on each other to be there in good times and bad. Both of you expect honesty and authenticity in your relationship. If you are contemplating a job or having problems in your family, you know you can count on him to listen to you and care that you are struggling. If you are feeling down, you know you can count on him to pump you up. The two of you know each other inside and out—the good, the bad, and the ugly—and you get along okay in spite of it.

You are both basically emotionally healthy individuals.

In my work with women, I have seen way too many relationships comprised of one strong individual and one unhealthy individual. Although the strong partner might enjoy taking care of the other and being in control of the relationship in the very beginning, this partnership never bodes well as time goes on. Eventually, one partner gets sick and tired of being the strength in the relationship and not having his or her own needs met. Another scenario I have witnessed is when the unhealthy partner becomes stronger and wants a voice in the relationship. While it is to be commended for a person to become stronger and healthier, the other partner might not positively receive this change. The partnership will be upset when the balance of power changes significantly.

You and your significant other challenge yourself and continue to grow as individuals over time.

In a long-term relationship, it is vital for each partner to continue to grow. It is easy to become comfortable and complacent because we *are* creatures of habit! It is much more difficult to continue to challenge ourselves to get outside our comfort zones. When one individual continues to grow, learn, and change over time while the other does not, it is difficult to keep the relationship fresh, exciting, and new.

You both know how to compromise to make a relationship work.

A great relationship requires two people to make it work. That means *you* don't do all the giving and *he* doesn't do all the taking! You each work equally hard to make the relationship work well. Each makes an effort to compromise at different times to make each other happy. Compromising does **NOT** mean giving up your identity or your most valued goals on a regular basis. What it *does* mean is that the relationship is yin and yang, give and take.

Partners in the relationship bring out the BEST in each other.

Do I really have to elaborate on this point? You know *that* couple when you see them: They're great apart, but they're even better together. They complement each other and are able to support and prod each other forward to achieve great things.

Partners in the relationship are able to clearly articulate to each other what they need to be happy!

SASS ALERT!!! If you can't do this yet, you have not found

your inner sass! Expecting your guy to figure out your needs is a waste of time that will end in disappointment and possibly a bad fight. But here's the deal: You need to own this one! If you want someone to give you what you want in life, you need to master this skill today. Find your voice, girlfriend! In my thirty years of marriage, I have learned that men are relieved and pleased when you tell them exactly what you need and want. It makes their lives much, much easier, and it will make yours much, much happier.

The key to good relationships is to truly know YOU! If you don't know who you are, what you want, what you need to be happy, where you want to be in life, or what your deal-breakers are, you will struggle in your relationships. Get to know yourself!!

Give it a Little More Thought, Girlfriend

1. Are you currently in a relationship? If so, how does it stack up according to the above guidelines for a great relationship?

_____

_____

_____

_____

_____

_____

2. What aspects of your relationship do you think need fine-tuning? What do you plan to do about it?

_____

_____

_____

_____

_____

_____

Your Call to Action

If you're currently in a relationship, try this exercise to connect better. Set aside twenty minutes each day, with no outside distractions, to talk to your significant other. Be sure you're both sitting in close proximity so you can look directly in each other's eyes while you are talking. Each partner should make a conscious effort to truly listen while the other speaks.

_____

_____

_____

_____

_____

_____

Business Sass for the Girlfriend

Relationships are not the only area in which we want to succeed. I bet you want to know the secret to success in the workplace, right? Well, the reality is this: Being successful requires a combination of skills, talents, smarts, and good old common sense! Read on, girlfriend, and learn how to get ahead and make your mark in the world.

Don't forget to use your instincts.

Believe it or not, your instincts are some of the most powerful tools in your arsenal. When you tap into your instincts and what just "feels right." you will automatically know when to move forward. when to cut your losses and move on to another job, whom you should trust and whom you definitely shouldn't, and so on. Some women have difficulty tapping into their instincts because they learned early on in their childhoods to override those feelings and not trust them. They've stopped listening to what they *feel* and simply jump headfirst into situations, ignoring the screeching warning emanating inside their own hearts and heads. My advice to you is to start listening—to YOU!

Take the temperature in the room.

Every girlfriend needs to understand the culture in her workplace to be successful. Each business environment has a different feel to it, a unique way of doing things, a set of unwritten rules. If you are new on the job, lie low for a while and observe your surroundings. Who are the successful and respected workers and why? Who gets promoted and why? Who is trustworthy, and who has a direct line to the boss? Knowing the answers to these questions is vital for your success on the job.

Be sure you understand the culture in your workplace! So, I hear through the grapevine that you want to move up at work. Congratulations on your ambition and drive to want more in life. Wait...you say you've been working incredibly hard, putting in an extraordinary number of hours, as well as energy and dedication, only to get passed over for a promotion? They gave it to someone else who didn't "deserve" it? I'm not surprised by this turn of events, but allow me to explain what I mean...

Girlfriends who get promoted establish positive relationships with people who have formal and informal power.

A sassy girlfriend has worked hard on establishing a good relationship with her supervisors. She has spent time understanding the culture of the organization and knows who has decision-making power, even though they do not necessarily have a prime parking spot, a placard on their office door, or a position that holds any formal power. I worked in a company where I quickly learned that the secretary had a direct line to the bosses. Her job went far beyond filing paperwork and fetching coffee: She actually had some say-so when it came to company decisions! This was valuable information that I was able to put to good use at a later date.

Girlfriends who get promoted have made a point of letting people see how great they are.

Now, this is a hard one for a lot of women. We don't always feel comfortable bragging about our achievements, but the reality is that it could be the key to you moving up in the world! All of your hard work will be in vain if you don't let others see how skilled and talented you are at your job. When you do anything that can be interpreted as positive, make sure your boss is aware of it. This is all about selling **YOU** in the best possible light. The woman sitting next to you might be doing the same caliber of work, but if her supervisor isn't weekly aware of how great she is, she will go unnoticed. Also, don't wait for your job evaluation to ask the boss how you are doing. Ask for feedback often so you know **exactly** where you stand and how you can improve and catch the boss's attention.

Network with EVERYONE in the organization. Get connected and known.

Make it a plan to meet and network with everyone you can. Join committees at your place of work and take part in as many work-oriented functions as possible. Approach your inter-actions with co-workers and superiors as one long job interview. The secret is to always keep your short- and long-term goals in mind as you navigate through your organization and your daily duties.

Girlfriends who get promoted know how to rock their talk.

I can't overemphasize how important your communica-tion skills are in the workplace! Being a good listener is the key to being successful in your job. If you are truly a good listener, you will better understand what your organization and the indi-viduals who work within it really expect and need from you, as well as what you need to do to succeed and climb the ladder like you deserve. Some girlfriends spend too much time talking and not enough time actually listening.

Sassy girlfriends don't bring their emotions to work with them.

It is important to keep in mind that employers are inter-ested in individuals who are capable of getting along with others and know how to handle difficult people. This enables them to have "fewer headaches" to deal with at work, since personnel management is likely one of their assigned tasks. You need to be one of *those* people; if you are a "hothead" or a "crybaby" or a "tattletale," you will definitely not fall into this category. Make it a point to be thoughtful, calm, and wise in the workplace. As you navigate your work life, it is inevitable that you will come across at least one co-worker who is a pain in your side—and maybe even your backside! As difficult as it might be, you must treat such interactions as an important learning experience and han-dle them with as much finesse as possible. Remember that what might feel good to say in a heated moment can forever hang over your head and impede you from getting that promotion you so desire.

Be sure to keep reasonable boundaries in your workplace.

I really can't say this enough: Setting and keeping good, reasonable boundaries is as essential in your professional life as it is in your personal life. Some girlfriends think they will be successful if they agree to everything their boss and co-workers ask them to do. Nothing could be further from the truth! This yes-woman technique will lead to exhaustion, frustration, and disrespect. Now don't get me wrong: You need to try to please your boss and impress him or her with your ability in the workplace. However, you need to know when to say "No." The company needs to see that you have a voice and that you know your limits. If you don't, you will be stepped on and passed over at work. In addition, if you think always saying "Yes" is the key to being promoted, you are sadly misinformed. The workhorse does not necessarily get the promotion in the end.

The bottom line is this: the key to being successful in the workplace goes way beyond just working hard. You need to work **strategically** and **smart.**

Biggest mistake girlfriends make in their lives? Not listening to their gut. Stop overriding your instincts! They are there to protect you and point you in the right direction in life.

Give it a Little More Thought, Girlfriend

1. Do you feel you do a good job marketing yourself at work? Why or why not?

_____

_____

_____

_____

_____

_____

2. Looking back at your job experience, have you ever been in a situation for which you wish you had a do-over? What would you do differently this time?

_____

_____

_____

_____

_____

_____

Your Call to Action

Make a list of the strengths, skills, and talents you're able to utilize at work on a daily basis. When you're finished, take a look at your list. Are you utilizing your true talent in the workplace? Be creative! Try to imagine ways in which you might further use your skills and talents in the workplace...and then go do it!

_____

_____

_____

_____

_____

_____

The Perfect Girlfriend Syndrome

Are you a girlfriend who thinks she needs to do everything to perfection in order to be successful? Women today are expected to be so many things to so many people. We are expected to be ambitious workers, perfect mothers, keep a beautiful home, have a great marriage, and give birth to exceptional children! Oh, and I forgot that we need to look great in the process! The reality of the situation is that the chances of being able to accomplish all of those things to perfection, all at the same time, are slim to none. Eventually, we'll hit a snag in the road. At some point in life, this label of perfection will become too heavy of a burden to carry and lug around, and it will get in the way of our happiness. We will have the constant feeling that we are failing to measure up in some way. So, how do we change our ways? Read on, girlfriend...

Have realistic expectations.

Accept that every aspect of your life is not always and doesn't have to be perfect to be good. At some point, you will run into obstacles to perfection: a down-cycle in your job, a child who disappoints you, a friend who is angry at you, or a husband who totally drops the ball in your marriage. This is called life, and no one makes it through without some heartaches. The important people in your life are not perfect either; they make plenty of their own mistakes. When your expectations are set so high, it is easy for everyone to disappoint you—even for *you* to disappoint you. Expecting your life to be flawless sets you up for one fall after another. Expecting your life to be flawless sets you up to be unhappy.

Reassess your priorities.

Do you volunteer your precious time for every committee at work or at your kid's school? Do you find yourself up late at night, baking cupcakes for someone or throwing together your child's costume for the school play? Give this one some thought: Do you have this subconscious need to prove to everyone (including yourself) that you can do it all? The reality is that no one can do it all and do it well. This, girlfriends, is a proven fact. Eventually, one of those plates you're spinning is going to come crashing to the ground and leave you feeling tired, frustrated, and unhappy, with nothing but a shattered mess to show for it. The solution to this dilemma is to reassess what is important to you in your life: simplify! For example, when my kids were young, I decided that spending quality time with them after I had worked all day was more important to me than serving an elaborate home-cooked meal. That became my priority, and I made peace with not being the perfect housekeeper and cook.

Differentiate between success and perfection.

Contrary to what you're thinking in your head right now, there is a way to be successful in life without being perfect. Need an example? Allow me to introduce...ME! I believe I'm successful in life, even though my life is far from perfect. If you open my dresser drawers, you will not find them neat and organized, as my husband can attest to—and in case you are wondering, I do not intend to change this in the near future. My sons made plenty of mistakes and were quite imperfect as teenagers, yet they are turning into successful, responsible adults. And guess what...they are still not perfect. In spite of their imperfections, I am still very proud of my skills as a parent. I don't cook nearly as much as I used to, yet I don't let it bother me. You know why? I've made a conscious decision to prioritize my time in other areas of my life.

Be authentic in your life.

Be honest, authentic, and genuine in everything you do and say. Part of the reason we get stuck on perfection is because we want to look "good" to other people. We want to impress others with our "perfectness" and be admired. At the root of this behavior is the need for us to feel better about ourselves, but the problem with this is that it actually doesn't make us feel better; in fact, it does the opposite, as it really doesn't work too well. Carrying on this perfection charade is hard on everyone, including you *and* the other people in your life.

One time, I was cooking in my kitchen with my friend. As I reached for the oregano in the spice cupboard, my friend started laughing. I didn't understand what was going on until she stated that she liked me much better after seeing the inside of my cupboard, which she assumed would be immaculately organized, alphabetized, and absolutely perfect. She felt I gave off an air that I had it "so together." I did, but that certainly didn't mean that my oregano had to be perfectly centered between the nutmeg and the paprika! You can look good without being perfect.

Everyone "messes up" now and then. It is how you respond to the mistake that changes you in life.

Give it a Little More Thought, Girlfriend

1. Are there times in your life when you've felt the perfection syndrome getting in the way of your happiness and healthiness? When?

_____

_____

_____

_____

_____

_____

2. Be honest: do you think you are realistic about your expectations of YOU?

_____

_____

_____

_____

_____

_____

Your Call to Action

Are there responsibilities in your daily routine that exist only for the sake of you being seen by others as perfect? Write them down and define a new goal that reflects a new and more reasonable expectation of self. For example: "I will no longer cook a full homemade dinner seven days a week for my family. I will only do this five days a week, and I will be fine with it." Keep track on paper as to how your change is going.

_____

_____

_____

_____

_____

_____

Live in the Moment, Girlfriend!

One of the major steps in finding your inner sass is perfecting the art of mindfulness. This is the ability to live in the moment and enjoy life without thoughts about the past or worries about the future. As you can imagine, mastering this skill takes hard work and focus, but it is more than worth it!

Let me give you an example: Let's imagine that a girlfriend is at her son's baseball game. While she's giving off the illusion of watching the game, she's actually busy making a mental list of the things she needs to accomplish the next day. She's worrying whether or not she'll have enough time to finish tomorrow's work proposal. At the same moment, she's thinking about what to wear to her big meeting and fretting that nothing will look good enough. Her thoughts then go to her sister and their unfortunate disagreement on the phone three weeks prior; she worries about whether her sister is still angry with her and how it might manifest itself at the following month's family reunion.

Now let's adjust the picture. Let's assume the same girlfriend has learned how to practice mindfulness and be fully present. She's at her son's baseball game, but that's where the similarities stop between the two scenarios. This girlfriend is enjoying the outdoors after sitting at her desk in her stuffy office. Fully present, she listens to the chatter of the game and hears the sounds of children playing in the park. She puts her face up to the sky to catch some rays of sunshine, smell the clean air, and hear the birds chirping. She watches as her son makes a great play at second base, and she enjoys the huge, accomplished smile on his face and makes one of her own to match it.

Guess what: Whether she worries about that proposal or not, she still has the same amount of time to finish it. Whether or not she frets about her clothes, she still has the same wardrobe to choose from for the big meeting. On top of that, there is no point wasting her time mulling over a three-week-old fight, ruminating about something she cannot take back, change, or control. The saddest part of the whole first scenario is that the mother could not even enjoy the excitement on her son's face as he made his great play. Come to think of it, she was supposed to be at the game to *watch* her son play, but her mind was a million other places.

Be able to define a "quality moment" you will remember.

I hate to admit this, but I was guilty of this behavior for many years. I was so intent on getting where I had to go and accomplishing my goals that I often missed the best and most memorable moments of my life. I was always planning the next thing or worrying about something that had transpired in the past. But then, it happened: <u>I started to notice that my kids were getting older, and it struck me that I needed to slow down and enjoy NOW.</u>

Now, I make it a habit to be in the moment. I learned how to recognize when I was having one of those rare life instances. For example, on vacation, my family went around the table and shared what they were most grateful for in life. As I listened to their answers, I froze the moment. Fully present, I recognized how lucky I was to have such a family in my life. I actually remember saying to myself, "This is one of those moments."

Mastering the art of living in the moment will change your life. From a physiological standpoint, it has the capability to reduce stress and anxiety and boost your body's immune functioning. It will greatly improve your relationships and make you much more effective at work. All of this will lead you to a much happier and healthier life.

If you find a lot of "should have," "could have," and "if only" in your conversations, you need to change your way of thinking. You have nothing to gain by indulging in these types of thought patterns of defeat. Girlfriend, accept the past; while you can't change it, you can learn from it. Take that knowledge and keep climbing the mountain!

Give it a Little More Thought, Girlfriend

1. Do you feel you practice the art of living in the moment? Why or why not?

_____

_____

_____

_____

_____

2. When is it hardest to stay present and focused on NOW? What can you do to change this behavior?

_____

_____

_____

_____

_____

Your Call To Action

We tend to breathe fast and take shallow breaths when we are anxious and stressed. Becoming aware of your breathing and slowing it down is the first step to controlling the stress and anxiety in your life. Master this deep-breathing exercise to relax your body and mind. You can practice this at work, at home, or even in line at the store when the person in front of you has 100 coupons, needs a price check, and wants to pay with a check!

Deep-Breathing Exercise: While sitting in a comfortable place, put one hand on your chest and one on your stomach. Take a long, deep breath in through your nose and count slowly to three in your head. You should feel the breath coming from deep within your stomach, not your chest. Exhale through your mouth, again counting "One...two...three." Concentrate on your breathing, feeling your stomach rise and fall with each deep breath.

How Many Suitcases are You Carrying?

Want to be a girlfriend who has found her inner sass? If so, you need to deal with your luggage right away. What am I talking about? I'm referring to all the baggage you carry with you daily. You might choose to believe that those emotional experiences from your past have nothing to do with you today, but the truth is that they negatively impact every aspect of your life. They color your interpretations every time you attempt to communicate with others. They hold you back from becoming the successful woman you yearn to be in life. The bottom line is this: That luggage stands in the way of you finding your inner sass.

I worked in an organization with a woman who lugged around a steamer trunk all day. Obviously, I don't mean this literally! Although she **was** extremely talented and smart, her luggage consistently got in the way of her success. One time, a meeting was called to clear up a few misunderstandings between the luggage carrier and myself. After some discussion, I surmised that this girlfriend felt threatened by me. Understanding that and wanting to defuse the situation, I complimented her, raving about a project she had created and implemented. Her reply? Anger! "Did you hear that? See what I mean? She just insulted me!" That was the moment when I knew nothing I said was going to make any difference to her. Why? Because it wasn't about me.

Her perception of the experience was colored by the baggage she had in her life. There were only three people who were physically in the meeting room that day; however, we were joined by a slew of ghosts from her past. See, girlfriends, when we haven't worked through the hurts, anger, and painful experiences from our previous years of living, they creep up on us when we least expect it. We have difficulty interpreting and understanding the true meaning in each experience without dragging the muck from our past into it. Apparently, this girlfriend had experienced criticism from a significant woman in her past. She replayed it time and time again with different individuals who ventured in and out of her life. The tape in her head was playing so loudly *that* day that it was impossible for her to view her life or any situation clearly.

I see this occur with many women who struggle in their intimate relationships. The baggage they carry around from their past relationships slowly seeps into the current one. This happens so effortlessly that they aren't even aware of its affect on their lives. They just keep replaying the same old hurts and wounds from their past and subconsciously incorporating them into their communication in the relationship. Without the self-awareness they need in order to change their behavior, the chances are slim that they will ever have a happy, healthy relationship.

If you have suitcases that have been getting heavier and heavier by the day, deal with it now, even if that means you have to get professional help. The luggage only gets more cumbersome over time. Take control of your life—past, present, and future—and you will be one step closer to finding your inner sass!

Having self-awareness is only the first step to finding happiness. The next step is using that self-awareness to deal with the issues and move forward in your life.

Give it a Little More Thought, Girlfriend

1. Is it possible that you have been carrying around some suitcases or baggage of your own? In what part of your life do you have some unfinished business?

_____

_____

_____

_____

_____

Can you think of a time when your luggage colored the way you handled a situation? What happened?

_____

_____

_____

_____

_____

Your Call to Action

Make a list of your baggage, the unfinished business that's weighing you down in life. How long have you lugged it around? It's time to finally let it go.

Hold a letting-go ceremony by taking the list of baggage and tearing the paper to shreds. As you do this, verbally state what you are letting go of and why letting it go will enable you to lead a happy, healthy life.

_____

_____

_____

_____

_____

_____

It's Just a Number, Girlfriend!

The interesting thing about celebrating birthdays is that you never feel like the age your driver's license states you are—or at least I don't. In my mind, I'm still a kid. In fact, sometimes I look in the mirror and ask myself, "When did that happen?" I truly don't feel old inside my head. That's why I'm always shocked when my body does not cooperate with my mind. Two years ago, I was struggling with back pain. At the orthopedic doctor's office, they performed an MRI and prescribed a strong anti-inflammatory medication, along with weekly physical therapy. When I saw the assessment sheet for my back at the doctor's office, I was somewhat shocked by my diagnosis: **degenerative disc disease.**

Apparently, it is a common effect of aging on the back, but I couldn't believe it. I was sure some sort of injury must have been the culprit for my back condition. Like I said before, in my head, I think I'm young. When I tell someone my age, the number say out loud always surprises me because it's certainly not how I truly feel.

Have you ever met someone very young who acts old? They don't look old per se, but their demeanor, their energy level, and their dress all personify the word. On the contrary, you may have met people who have many years behind them but give off a very young vibe. They come across as having energy, dress very trendy and stylish, and are knowledgeable about the world, technology, and pop culture. People enjoy being around these people, and they enjoy being around people of different ages. What I'm trying to say here is something you've probably heard before: Age ain't nothin' but a number!

I have a girlfriend who's trying to decide what to do with the rest of her life. She has already dedicated many years to raising her children and working at home. An extremely intelligent woman, she is capable of whatever she sets her mind to. She shared that she would like to go back to school now that the kids are out of the house, but her special area of interest would take her four years to complete. In other words, if she goes back to school, she will be X number of years old by the time she finishes with her degree. She feels she will be too old by then to start practicing in her area of interest, and she'll probably want to spend more time with her family by then. In essence, she feels it's not worth it at this point in life to move toward this goal.

Here are my thoughts on this subject: Whether she goes back to school or not, there's no way around the fact that she is going to be the same age in four years! She is sitting back in life and waiting for her family to get to the point where they can spend time with her, but hasn't she already spent her whole life doing that? Didn't she already put her own life on hold so others could accomplish their goals? Isn't it time she just move forward on her own goals, regardless of her age?

A woman named Nola Oches graduated at the age of ninety-eight with a master's degree. I'm going to assume Nola didn't give much thought as to whether she would be too old when she graduated or whether it was even worth the trouble to go back to school. I have seen the picture of Nola at her graduation, and she seems pretty proud and pleased with herself. Personally, I believe Nola has the right idea. She isn't living her last years "waiting" for something to happen.; rather, she's making things happen and accomplishing more goals. Nola is my kind of girlfriend, and I think we could all agree that Nola has found her inner sass.

Girlfriend motto to staying young:
- *View life as an adventure!*
- *Push yourself to learn new skills and take on new goals throughout your lifetime.*
- *Let go of the baggage and focus on what is truly important in life!*

Give it a Little More Thought, Girlfriend

1. What one thing would you do in your life if you were twenty years younger? Why can't you achieve this now?

_____

_____

_____

_____

_____

2. Why do you think Nola went back to school? What's one unaccomplished goal that's hanging over your head?

_____

_____

_____

_____

_____

_____

Your Call to Action

Develop a bucket list. Brainstorm and be open to whatever comes into your mind. Write down a concrete plan as to how you can fulfill each one of these goals.

_____

_____

_____

_____

_____

_____

Change it Up, Girlfriend!

Is there a part of your life you would love to change, but you just feel stuck? Do you know in your heart that you would be happier if you could just move forward, yet you stay where you are? Everyone, at some point in their life, struggles with moving on and changing it into the one that they truly want. Like it or not, you are making a decision when you make no decision: You resist change. But why do we do this to ourselves?

Fear can stop you in your tracks.

One reason you're having difficulty moving forward is fear. Maybe it's fear of the unknown. Even if you're unhappy right now, you know what to expect with life if you keep everything exactly the same. Who cares if you're miserable? You'd rather be miserable because it's familiar! Yes, that's right! Some women get so comfortable with being miserable that they don't even realize there's a whole different and better way to live life! There's a comfort level in keeping things status quo because you definitely know what to expect. You have no idea how things could turn out if you change your life, and that, girlfriend, can be terrifying. But on the other hand, it can also be very exciting. It's possible that you have forgotten how great it feels to take a risk and put yourself out there. This is especially true if you've gotten comfortable in your small world and haven't ventured outside of it for quite a while. But growing and changing is what life is really all about. Gather up your courage and take a leap of faith!

Try something different, girlfriend.

Let me throw another reason out there as to why you can't move forward: You have attempted this change before and failed. Because of this bad experience, you assume any further attempts will be futile. Failure is painful, and you don't want to feel it again. But guess what, girlfriend: That excuse is just not good enough. Not everyone succeeds on their first try or even their second. It just means you need to try again. Maybe you need to change your approach or tweak the process a bit. It certainly doesn't mean things can't change, and it certainly doesn't mean you should keep trying the same thing over and over if it doesn't work! It just means you haven't found the right recipe yet. Change the ingredients and try again.

You think you have something to gain by staying in your current situation.

THERE **IS** A PAY-OFF FOR YOU STAYING JUST WHERE YOU ARE RIGHT NOW! That's right, be honest with yourself. If you stay in your current situation, as bad as it seems, what are you gaining? Maybe you have a lot of drama and chaos in your life, and maybe there is a part of you that finds this enjoyable. Also, it might enable you to garner a lot of attention from your friends. I hope you see my point, as you need to be brutally honest with yourself to understand what is holding you back from making a positive change.

Your ability to change your situation always goes back to knowing YOU. If you gain a better understanding of what's beneath the surface, you can increase your chances of making strides in your quest to change your life. Without this awareness, it will be difficult for you to gain traction on your goals. Once you understand your own motives, you can face it and deal with courage. Girlfriends, discover what is holding you back. Face your fears and achieve your dreams!

Hey, girl, you want change? Then stop talking about it and do it. Stop trying to convince everyone—including you—that it can't happen. You can do anything you set your mind to. Think positive and keep pushing forward.

Give it a Little More Thought, Girlfriend

Are you contemplating a change in your life but struggling with moving forward? Maybe the following questions will help jump-start your new life. Think of a part of your life that you would like to change. Take your time and be brutally honest in your answers.

1. What one thing do you want to change in your personal or professional life?

We always have certain aspects of our lives that we want to improve. What is it in your life? Is it your career or something in your personal life? Do you want to become healthy physically and emotionally?

_____

_____

_____

_____

_____

_____

2. Have you attempted to change before now? What have you tried?

Have you tried to change in the past but failed? What did you try that didn't work out? Look at the different methods you used and analyze whether they were the best solutions for your change. Could they be improved upon?

_____

_____

_____

_____

_____

_____

3. What are the benefits to you if you make this change?

How will your life change positively if you meet your challenge? What will be available to you if you achieve your goal? Try to visualize what your life will look like.

_____

_____

_____

_____

_____

4. What are the pay-offs for staying exactly where you are?

This may seem like a strange question, but the reality is this: You wouldn't stay where you are unless there was some benefit to staying where you are! Do some deep thinking on the subject and uncover why you might want to stay in the same place.

_____

_____

_____

_____

_____

_____

5. Why do you think you are struggling with this change?

Again, this question requires some inner probing. How does this change relate to the rest of your life? Why would this change be so difficult for you?

_____

_____

_____

_____

_____

_____

6. How would you feel about yourself if you made this change?

Again, visualize achieving your goal and imagine the feeling you would have at that moment. How would it feel? Write down the adjectives to describe how you would feel.

_____

_____

_____

_____

_____

_____

7. How do you feel about yourself staying where you are in life?

Be honest. How would you really feel if you didn't move from where you are right now? Write down the adjectives that come to mind.

_____

_____

_____

_____

_____

_____

Are you someone who makes things happen or do things just happen to you? The difference is the key to the happiness and success in your life.

Do You Have a Backseat Driver in Your Head?

Have you been hijacked by the driver in the backseat? When I say "backseat driver," I'm referring to the toxic thoughts that continuously flow through your head. You might not even be aware that this dialogue is taking place inside your brain, but if you listen carefully, you will hear it.

There you are, trying to steer your life in the right direction, when suddenly, your backseat driver, that inner critic, begins taking the wheel, steering you completely off course. Without your knowledge, it's reminding you of all the things that you're doing wrong in your life, instead of what you're doing right. Just when you need the most encouragement, your backseat driver spews toxic venom, destroying your self-esteem. Here's the ugly truth: Backseat drivers rarely show you how great you are. They are, however, true masters at knocking you down in life!

These automatic thoughts can be downright irrational at times.

In spite of this, there's a good chance that you will listen to what the backseat driver has to say and believe every word. Do you want an example? Let's say you just came out of a job interview. The interview went great, and you are excited about the opportunity. Your supervisor tells you she'll call you back within three days. Early in the third day, you begin to question yourself and your abilities. By the fourth day, you are already worrying, and by the fifth day, your backseat driver goes to work. Somewhere deep in your brain, these are your streaming thoughts: "I said all the wrong things. Why did I ask that last question? I'm so stupid! I totally blew it. They'll never promote anyone like me. That job would be way out of my league anyway. I'm definitely not good enough. I don't deserve that job. It's no wonder she didn't even bother calling me"

Does this sound familiar? Every girlfriend has experienced this at some point in her life. You can take quite a beating without ever stopping to think objectively or rationally about the situation. So let's look at some perfectly reasonable explanations for not receiving a call back: Maybe the boss had an emergency at work that took priority over the hiring process, or maybe the job was put on hold because they are not hiring anymore. It's possible that she was told to choose someone more affordable, or maybe a past "star employee" came back in the picture. The point is that there are numerous explanations for this scenario that have *absolutely* nothing to do with your abilities and skill level. Yet the backseat driver just takes off and goes right for your Achilles heel, your confidence and self-esteem.

What can you do to stop your backseat driver?

First, you need to learn to become aware of these thoughts as they are happening. Usually, we don't even pay attention to the chatter in the background; we just get used to it because it's always been there. Try really hard to hone in on what is being said and make a point to turn the negative thought that runs through your mind into a positive. This is a skill and *will* take time and perseverance. Remember, if your backseat driver has been working in overdrive since the day you were born, you're not going to turn everything around in the span of a day. For example, if your thought is, "I'm just not good at this job," reframe this thought to something like: "I'm doing as well as can be expected at this point in my training, and I'll improve every day."

The most important reason you need to take your backseat driver seriously: Your thoughts influence your actions.

If you listen and buy in to some of this toxic chatter on a regular basis, you will act and behave accordingly. Just imagine that you're in an unhealthy relationship with a controlling man. Your backseat driver is veering down a dangerous path with the following toxic thoughts: "I'm no good. I probably can't get anyone else but him. I can't make it on my own, so I have to stay in this situation. I don't deserve any better than this. He really isn't that bad. He needs me, so I can't leave him." If you begin to buy into this chatter, these toxic thoughts will drive you to stay in a relationship that is bad for you and going nowhere. **Your back-seat driver will distort your thinking to the point where you believe you have no options. Therefore, your thoughts will influence your actions!**

Let's review some of the ways you can distort your thinking.
Are you one of those girlfriends who sees everything in black and white? Do you believe there are no gray areas in any situations, that it's always all or nothing? For example, if you don't get 100 percent on your exam, you feel you did not perform well. Never mind that you just received a 96 percent; you still view this as a failure. Are you guilty of over-generalizing in your head? For example, "I always fail at staying on my diet, so why will this time be any different?" Are you searching out negative information and downplaying anything remotely positive? If this sounds vaguely familiar, then it might behoove you to work on the exercise on the next page.

Girlfriends, do yourself a favor and make a pact to kick that backseat driver out of your head once and for all!

Are you your own worst enemy? Are you hard on yourself to the point that you beat yourself up verbally? And the more you get going, the worse it gets? If you are not careful, after a while, you'll believe the distortions your backseat driver is throwing at you. Stop this destructive behavior! Start answering yourself as your trusted friend would. It works!

Give it a Little More Thought, Girlfriend

1. Have you had experiences in which you felt your backseat driver was getting in the way of your happiness and health? When?

_____

_____

_____

_____

_____

2. Are there times when you've felt your backseat driver has influenced your decisions in life? Describe those experiences.

_____

_____

_____

_____

_____

_____

Your Call to Action

On a piece of paper, keep track of the automatic thoughts that swirl through your head during the day. At the end of the day, take a look at the statements you've written down. Are there any negative remarks/thoughts on the page? If there are, try to replace them with more rational, positive statements. Become more aware of the chatter that's destroying your confidence...and do something about it!

_____

_____

_____

_____

_____

_____

Tap Into Your Instincts, Girlfriend!

Have you ever taken a test and instinctively answered the questions, only to go back over the test, over-think and over-analyze the questions, and change your initial answers? The changed answers usually are wrong, aren't they? Have you ever worked on a group project and just KNOWN that the group was going down the wrong path to find the answer? You couldn't really explain it, but you knew it wasn't going to work. How about meeting someone new and just sensing something negative about the person, even if it couldn't be reasoned out? These are all perfect examples of using your instincts.

Your instincts are nature's way of making sure you avoid harmful situations. They exist to protect you from physical and emotional danger. That hunch you have can't be explained and reasoned out, yet you know, time and time again, that it's right.

Working in the mental health field, I've come across women who consistently fail to use their instincts in their everyday life. They walk blindly into dangerous situations and then wonder how they got there. They ask, "How did this happen to me? Why didn't I see this man would be bad for me? Why didn't I catch the clues?" The answer seems to lie in the fact that they fail to do a gut check. They ignore the signs, possibly because they so desperately want things to work out, or maybe they lost touch with their self and their own needs years ago, growing up in a household where they were denied and were trained to ignore their instincts.

Recently, I was at the airport with my family, leaving on a vacation. There was a costumed character there for photos with travelers and tourists, and my husband decided we should have a picture taken with him. My husband, my two sons, my son's girlfriend, and I posed for the photo. Mr. Character positioned himself between my son's girlfriend and me. Immediately, I felt a sense of alarm and discomfort. Streaming through my head was the thought that the costumed person was making me feel very uncomfortable. I was relieved when the picture was over and I could pull away. As he walked away, my son's girlfriend whispered to me, "I couldn't wait to get away from him. That guy really gave me the creeps."

Apparently, we both tapped into our instincts and decided that something just didn't feel right. I've found in my personal and professional life that my instincts have never steered me wrong. What HAS steered me wrong in my life is over-thinking a situation and making a decision based only on facts.

I'm always surprised when I come across successful women who don't use their instincts in their professional lives. Recently, I worked with someone who fell into this category; she was very successful in business, but she based every single decision on facts and figures, 100 percent. I encouraged her to stretch outside her comfort zone and tap into her ability to sense things that are not based on facts. The very next week, she informed me of a situation in which she used her intelligence with a little gut sense thrown in! Here's the real secret to success: You will be unstoppable if you use your smarts coupled with your gut feelings. Ask any extraordinarily successful woman, and she will tell you that the combination of the two is the key to truly finding success.

So here's the answer to truly finding your inner sass in life: Tap into your instincts! Learn to trust that first feeling you get in a situation. Don't second-guess yourself and intellectualize the feeling. Just go with it and trust your gut!

The biggest mistake girlfriends make in life is not listening to their gut feelings. Stop overriding your instincts! They are there to protect you and point you in the right direction in life.

Give it a Little More Thought, Girlfriend

1. Name a time when you used your instincts in your personal or professional life.

_____

_____

_____

_____

2. Have there been times in your life where you second-guessed yourself and it worked against you?

_____

_____

_____

_____

Your Call to Action

Write down on a piece of paper a situation when you used your instincts. Take a few moments to visualize the experience and tap into the feelings you had at that moment in time. Can you name what some of those specific feelings or emotions were? Did your body exhibit a physical reaction during the experience?

_____

_____

_____

_____

_____

Boundaries for the Healthy Girlfriend

Everyone—and I mean *everyone*—could count on Mary. She was a great wife to Larry, a mother to three great kids, a doting daughter to her parents, and a devoted sister to her siblings. Mary worked a full-time forty-hour work week that often stretched out to fifty or sixty hours a week because Mary's boss knew he could count on her to take on the projects others were unwilling to do. She babysat her neighbor's kids on a weekly basis to help their mother out with her own busy life, but that neighbor never seemed interested in paying her for her valuable time or repaying the favor. Mary held a position in the school PTO and volunteered for several of its projects. The school could always count on Mary when they needed someone to bake or do just about anything no one else wanted to do.

Mary was a wonderful wife. When she got home from work, she made sure her family had homemade dinner. She set the table, served her family, and handled cleaning up afterward. Larry didn't do much; Mary was fine taking care of all of it herself because she knew he worked really hard. Larry's responsibility entailed washing his hands for dinner and sitting down to eat.

Mary was also a wonderful friend, and numerous women depended on her to solve their life issues. For some reason, every one of her friends seemed to be in a crisis on a regular basis. In fact, Mary had just been up until two a.m. on a weeknight with Anne, who was having a meltdown about her latest of many chaotic relationships. You could say that drama seemed to swirl around Anne. She knew she could always count on Mary to truly <u>feel</u> her pain and solve her problems.

The real problem was that everyone could count on Mary—except Mary! Mary usually thrived on helping others; it defined who she was as a person. But eventually, she began to feel an undercurrent of frustration and anger—feelings that were bubbling up in her, even though she couldn't understand why. She prided herself on being kind, helpful, and always there for everyone, but this new feeling took her by surprise. Unkind thoughts swirled through her head and scared her. She felt that her husband took advantage of her, her boss abused her kindness, and her kids walked all over her. Her friends and family were sucking the life out of her.

Do you feel like Mary sometimes? The problem that Mary struggled with was really a lack of personal boundaries. What are boundaries? They are what protect you and keep you safe in your relationships. They help you set up emotional fences—albeit invisible ones—in your life to keep you sane and healthy. Every girlfriend needs strong, well-defined boundaries in her life if she is going to survive and thrive. Girlfriends with boundaries know who they are and what they need to be happy and healthy in life.

If I were to name the biggest problem women struggle with, it would be the inability to maintain strong boundaries in their lives. Too many people view life with an all-or-nothing mentality and think saying "No" to someone's request means you aren't a kind person. But here's the scoop: If you have to sacrifice your own values and needs in life, you need to do some hard thinking. Many times, women mistakenly think there are only two adjectives to describe how they feel: They're either being *selfless* (which is appropriate in their minds) or *selfish*. They find it impossible to view all the shades of gray between these two descriptors, and they find it difficult to believe that it's acceptable and healthy to make a decision where you are being good to YOU!

What does it look like when a girlfriend has healthy boundaries in her life?

- She knows who she is at her core and what she needs to

be happy and healthy in life.

- She knows her limits; she will say "no" in a diplomatic manner when she feels it is healthy for her to do so.

- She has values and won't compromise them to try to please others.

- She surrounds herself with people who support her and her choice to be emotionally healthy.

- She distances herself from relationships that are toxic and not healthy for her.

- While getting to know someone new, she shares personal information slowly and appropriately.

- Her friendships are give-and-take relationships where each recognizes each other's needs.

- She has a good sense of balance in her life and realizes that she can't be everything to everyone.

- She recognizes her husband's, children's, and friends' problems as "their issues" to solve and does not take ownership of them.

- She allows her children to have their own identity and encourages them to be independent.

- She has a voice, and she doesn't hesitate to speak her mind when the situation calls for it.

- She has her own identity and insists on a loving relationship that will enable and encourage her to be challenged and grow.

- She understands and accepts that she won't be "liked" by everyone if she has strong healthy boundaries in her life. At some point, she will be told she's letting someone down, but she's okay with that.

- She has clearly defined rules in her house and doesn't cave in to her children's demands.

- As an adult, she understands that she doesn't have to respect others who show her absolutely no respect.

The bottom line is this: Girlfriends, having boundaries is KEY to living a healthy, happy life. A lack of boundaries will affect every aspect of your life and will definitely hold you back from finding your inner sass!

You are never going to make everyone happy. Accept this and move on. Making everyone happy does not equate with being a "good person." Good women, emotionally healthy women, and women with values don't always please people.

Give it a Little More Thought, Girlfriend

1. Was there any part of Mary's story that sounded familiar to you? What aspect of boundaries do you struggle with?

_____

_____

_____

_____

_____

_____

2. What changes can you make in your life to strengthen your boundaries in this area? Make a list of ways you can change your daily life to set and hold to boundaries.

_____

_____

_____

_____

_____

_____

3. Why do you think you struggle with this one area? In other words, what is the pay-off for not having these boundaries in your life?

_____

_____

_____

_____

_____

_____

4. How would your life improve if you had these boundaries?

_____

_____

_____

_____

_____

_____

Your Call to Action

Write down a specific boundary that you would like to improve in your life. Now, write a specific plan as to how you will accomplish this boundary change. Make sure to include the changes you will have to make on a daily basis. For example, if you'd like to start saying "NO" to requests when you don't have the time to fulfill them, write down some reasonable but firm statements you could make to the party who is demanding help. If you are struggling with this, ask a friend to help you.

_____

_____

_____

_____

_____

_____

Is Your Glass Half-Full?

Did you know that 20 percent of your outlook on life is genetic? You know what that means, don't you? You, girlfriend, have control of 80 percent of your outlook on life! This means we have the ability to *positively* control our attitude the majority of the time. Personally, I like these odds.

I am what you would call an eternal optimist in life. Whatever the situation, I always assume that everything is going to turn out great, and this attitude has served me well in life. While others during my business career said it was impossible to accomplish a task and encouraged me to not even try, I saw it as a challenge. If you want something bad enough and are persistent, it will happen. I know and sincerely believe we give off a positive energy when we trust that good things will happen.

What's comical about all of this is the fact that my husband is a pessimist by nature. I believe he genetically falls into this category and doesn't always use his own power to discourage this perspective. Even so, I think it can be quite effective for an eternal optimist to be married to a less-than-eternal optimist. Together, we make pretty decent parents and some pretty sound decisions.

I once had a client who affirmed my belief in positive energy. Every time we met, she talked about the many horrible issues in her life. When she walked in the room, it was as if she was enveloped in a gray cloud. Week after week, more bad things seemed to happen. She had a car accident and lamented that she didn't have a car. She hated her job, but she never bothered to look for a different one. She had alienated all of her friends, yet she complained about her lack of friendship. She had very bad luck with men in her life, and she always chose the ones who seemed destined to make her miserable. On top of that, her physical health was in decline. We discussed these problems in detail, and it was extremely difficult for her to see how things could get any better. She just assumed more bad things were going to happen. She lived her life believing she had very bad luck and that life was going to be unfair to her. If something bad could happen, she assumed it would happen to her. And guess what: More bad things kept happening. It was a self-fulfilling prophecy; what she expected to happen did indeed happen!

I know some people refuse to think positively because they're fearful of being disappointed if things don't work out in their favor. I believe this was at work in the above story. She didn't want to go out on a limb and risk thinking her life could possibly be any better because chances were, it wouldn't be. For her, it was safer to think things were going to stay the way they always were: gray. That way, she had much more to complain about to the few remaining people in her life who would listen, and she wasn't at all disappointed or surprised with the outcome.

My advice to you, girlfriend, is this: Think positive! Live life with your glass half-full. Believe that with hard work and perseverance and the right attitude in your personal and professional life, you can make anything happen. Positive energy is magnetic; it attracts more positive things into your life.

Make your own good luck in life. If you give off positive energy, you will get back positive energy. Assume that good things will happen to you!!

Give it a Little More Thought, Girlfriend

1. Would you say you are a positive thinker, or is your glass half-empty? How have you demonstrated this fact?

_____

_____

_____

_____

_____

2. Think back to your childhood and growing up. Did your parents see the glass half-full or half-empty? Do you see similarities to your own outlook?

_____

_____

_____

_____

_____

_____

Your Call to Action

Think about a goal you are trying to reach in your life. Maybe it's job success, losing weight, or quitting smoking. Now, close your eyes and imagine how your life will be once you achieve your goal. Be as specific and detailed as possible in your visualization. Try to incorporate all the positive feelings you will have when you acquire this goal. See your life as a movie in your mind, enjoying your accomplishments. See all the possibilities you will have in your new life.

Try to practice this visualization as much as possible; it will become easier the more you practice. The exercise will help you develop your positive thinking.

_____

_____

_____

_____

_____

_____

Steer Clear of Toxic People, Girlfriend!

So, you've made the decision to be healthy in your life. You are determined to eat right, exercise, and work toward your career goals. You are dedicated to living this new lifestyle and putting the past in the past. Going forward, you want to focus on your dreams. It's possible that now, there is only one thing standing between you and your dream life: **TOXIC PEOPLE!**

Do you allow toxic people into your life? They could be lurking in your family, circle of friends, or in your workplace. They can wreak havoc on your life just when you think you're finally at a point where you're moving forward. It seems as if certain girlfriends are magnetically pulled toward toxic individuals. They welcome them into their lives with open arms, ignoring the obvious clues that others see so clearly. How can they fail to notice the toxic individuals' blatant dysfunction? There seems to be no escape from this attraction as they forge ahead, doing nothing to discourage the relationship.

How do you know if you are entering a "toxic zone"? Take a look at these characters. Do they sound familiar? Remember, they might represent men, women, and family members in your life!

Instant Ivan

Ivan wants to be in a relationship with you way too fast. He will share intimate details of his life way before it's appropriate. Ivan could really use a crash course on having healthy boundaries. He will pressure you into becoming a staple in his life and will constantly want to know what is going on in yours. Whether it is a romantic relationship or just a friendship, be wary of anyone who wants to speed up the process. Healthy relationships and friendships grow over a period of time and through various life experiences.

Drama Debbie

Drama and chaos just swirls around this girlfriend. She will call you day and night to rant about yet another crisis in her life. Her world is **always** falling apart, and she doesn't know how to fix anything. The fascinating thing about Debbie is that she consistently puts herself in more situations that attract more drama and chaos, yet says she has no idea why these things keep happening to her. You will exhaust yourself trying to help her change her life, which she has no interest in doing! If you don't watch it, you will end up being in the middle of her chaos and drama.

Needy Nelly

She will call you all the time, always **desperately** needing your help. Nelly is not a strong person, and she makes really poor decisions. Time and time again, she proves herself to be weak and vulnerable and claims she needs your expert advice. The thing is, she never takes your expert advice, which means you become frustrated and exhausted trying to steer her in the right direction. This is a one-way friendship because Nelly is not capable of being there for you. In this scenario, you become an enabler, never allowing Nelly to learn how to stand on her own two feet.

Critical Cory

Cory can be a very smooth operator. Most of the time, he appears to be very kind, thoughtful, and sweet. When you least expect it, though, he will say something to you and you won't know how to take it. You will question yourself: "Did I just get insulted and criticized?" The bottom line is that Cory's manipulative and quite passive-aggressive in his relationships. He can't be trusted and certainly can't be counted on to be supportive of your endeavors. Cory is someone who will take advantage of any vulnerability or weakness. Be careful what you share with him because it won't stay between the two of you! This can be a family member, a co-worker, or even a friend.

Negative Ned

Let's face facts: It's hard to be around Ned. Whatever great idea you develop, he finds a reason that it will never work. If you talk excitedly about your plans for the weekend, Ned finds a way to extinguish your happiness. When you speak about your new boyfriend, Ned reminds you that the relationship is doomed for failure. Ned's glass is consistently half-empty, and he wants the same for you. You feel sorry for Ned because while he's basically a nice guy, his negativity in everything sucks the energy out of everyone around him. Ned is miserable in life, and he wants to share his misery with all those who surround him. Ned is toxic for you to the tenth degree!

Possessive Patsy

Patsy can be a good friend, but at times, her possessiveness can get on your nerves. She does not want you to have any other friends or people in your life. If you start dating someone, she will definitely not like him, and she will find every reason she can why the guy is not right for you. If you go to the movies with Mom, Patsy will be livid that she wasn't invited to go along. She will find subtle things wrong with every other person in your life and will constantly remind you why she is the only one who is really there for you. Patsy's great need in life is for you to be indebted to her. She craves for you to need her as much as she needs you.

Judgmental Jackie

Basically, Jackie thinks it's always her way or the highway! If you don't think like her, there must be something wrong with *you*. She easily discounts anyone who doesn't agree with her and is extremely judgmental of people that you think are just wonderful. Jackie is condescending and can be downright mean to others. She is very particular about whom she is willing to let into her circle and is also very quick to kick you to the curb if you don't follow her rules. Jackie's love for you is conditional: You'll have a great relationship with her, as long as you do exactly what she says. She is not the type to say "I'm sorry," so forget about her owning up to any responsibility or apologizing for anything.

Now that you know what to look out for, how can you avoid these dysfunctional people? It's simple:

Allow others to take on responsibility for their own lives. Solving their problems is not your job! You can't save anyone who doesn't try to save themselves; only they can change their own lives. Don't enable others to continue their dysfunctional behavior.

Remember that you need to take care of YOU first. If anyone infringes on your ability to be happy and healthy, you need to distance yourself from that person. This includes family members who inhibit your chance of leading a healthy life.

Remind yourself that a relationship—even with a family member—is supposed to be a two-way street. In other words, an emotionally healthy relationship requires give and take. You both take turns supporting each other through the ups and downs of life. Each member of the relationship has an obligation to demonstrate respect, and this includes parents.

- **If you are** unable to just be yourself when you are with someone, that is a sign that you are in the presence of a toxic person.

- **If you are** exhausted and stressed when you are around that person, that is a sign that you are in the presence of a toxic person.

- **If you are** dreading to be with that person but you do it anyway, that is a sign that you are in the presence of a toxic person.

- **If you are** unsure and uneasy as to how the person will react from day to day, that is a sign that you are in the presence of a toxic person.

- **If you are** carefully monitoring your words on a regular basis so as not to upset that person, that is a sign you are in the presence of a toxic person.

- **If you are** always giving that person another chance, that is a sign that you are in the presence of a toxic person.

- **If you are** constantly making excuses for that person's behavior, that is a sign that you are in the presence of a toxic person.

Have you allowed toxic people into your life? These are the ones who cause chaos around you, upset you, and keep you from feeling balanced and emotionally healthy. These people come with plenty of drama. Take an inventory of the people in your life and decide which ones add to your life and which ones take away from your happiness and health.

Give it a Little More Thought, Girlfriend

1. Take an inventory of the people in the various facets of your life: workplace, family, friends, etc. Separate them into two groups; list those who make a positive impact and add to your life and make another list of those who are negative and take away from your happiness and emotional health.

_____

_____

_____

_____

_____

2. Now, let's focus on the negative list.

a. Why do you keep this person in your life? (What is the pay-off for you?)

_____

_____

_____

_____

_____

b. How can you decrease the amount of time and energy you invest in this relationship?

_____

_____

_____

_____

_____

_____

3. Now that you have identified the toxicity in your life, create a daily plan to decrease your time, energy, and emotional investments in this relationship.

_____

_____

_____

_____

_____

_____

Rock Your Talk, Girlfriend!

When my kids were growing up, I always knew when they were not telling me the whole truth. I remember it like it was yesterday: They would stand in front of me, looking directly into my eyes in all their alleged innocence, and explain their very plausible story. I always managed to call their bluff, to the point where my boys believed I had some special gift that enabled me to see what others were incapable of seeing. Actually, they thought I had eyes in the back of my head. The reality was that I simply knew how to really listen.

Generally speaking, most people are lousy listeners. First, let's review some basics. Did you know that about 55 percent of the communicated message is understood through our nonverbal cues? How about the fact that 38 percent of the message is picked up from the tone of your voice? That means only a measly 7 percent of your message is communicated by the actual words you speak. On the flipside, if you aren't focusing intently on the individual during the communication process, it's very easy to miss the whole meaning of the message!

Think about the world we live in today, girlfriend. Multitasking is a way of life for most of us. In fact, we wear that skill like a badge of honor! If you're checking your e-mail and listening to someone at the same time, you can easily miss the intended message. If you're texting and listening to someone at the same time, you can easily miss out on what the speaker is saying. If you're thinking about what you might wear tomorrow while talking with someone, chances are pretty good you will miss a part of the message. You might pick up the basic gist of the conversation, but you can miss the subtle meaning behind the words used.

The other day, I was having a discussion with my husband about an e-mail I had received from a friend. I explained to him why I was upset about the e-mail, and then I read it to him out loud, inserting my own tone and inflection into the note. He looked at me for a while and then read it back to me, inserting a very different tone that changed the whole meaning of the e-mail. This made me realize just how difficult it is to make sure others derive the intended meaning of our written communication. It also really hit home how careful we need to be with our communication when it isn't face to face.

Girlfriends, here's the deal: The person sending the message comes into the communication process with a whole world of expectations, experiences, and perceptions. These are very different than the expectations, experiences, and perceptions of the receiver. Obviously, this makes it difficult for sent messages to be received in the intended manner. Just think about how each person in the world is so different and how all of their unique experiences have shaped their world. Now, just imagine how easy it is for the message to be misconstrued! If you aren't focusing intently on the individual during the communication process, it's easy to miss the whole meaning of the message!

If you need an example of a good listener, pay attention. Many years ago, I attended a school meeting held by the superintendent, and I sat in the back half of the room. The meeting lasted about an hour and covered the goals and challenges for the following year. It is important to note that I really didn't know any of the sixty people in the room, including the superintendent, but I listened to him and didn't ask any questions. As I was walking out of the room at the end of the meeting, the superintendent stopped me. He introduced himself and said that as he was talking, he could see that I was questioning some of what was being discussed. I was floored! He had noticed me among the sea of people and read the expressions on my face. Now, those were some exceptional listening skills! The fact that he stopped me to clarify my stance on the topic of discussion further revealed his gift as a communicator. Are your listening skills that sharp?

Another important question is: Do you realize all the ways you can communicate? In a workshop I gave on communication, I asked the participants to write down all the ways we can send a message. They had things on their lists that I hadn't even considered. To say I was impressed would be an understatement. That experience reminded me of the importance of remembering the role of your appearance, facial expressions, body movements, and touch in sending a message out to others about YOU!

If you want to find your inner sass, you need to become an awesome communicator, girlfriend! Heed the following tips on perfecting your skills:

- Technology plays an important part in our lives today. Make a point to unplug when someone is speaking with you. Nothing irritates me more than a girlfriend who sits there texting away during a meeting. In doing so, she sends a clear message to others that she does not respect their time.

- When you're holding a conversation, be sure to look the person directly in the eyes. The eyes and face can reveal so much of what the person is trying to convey. I often find the true message in the facial expressions of my colleagues rather than the actual words being said.

- Focus on what is presently being said in the conversation instead of thinking about what you're going to say next. At times, we are all guilty of this sin! We are so intent on saying the right thing to the other individual that we miss what is actually being said to us.

- Pay attention to the body language of the individual with whom you are communicating. So much of the message can be revealed in their stance, the way they hold their body, if they talk with their hands, or spatial distance.

- Don't forget that the tone of a person's voice plays an important part in the communication process. From the tone, you can surmise if someone is angry with you! They could be using words that seem friendly, but their tone will give their true feelings away.

- Remember that a person's past experiences can color the way the message is conveyed. This is why it is crucial to pay attention to their nonverbal responses. Baggage can greatly influence both how we convey and how we receive messages. I can't repeat this enough.

- If you want to be an awesome communicator, minimize any judgments or emotions in your interactions. Leave your emotions out of the communication process, especially at work, or they will severely hamper your ability to be an effective communicator.

- Keep in mind what it is that is motivating the other person in the communication exchange. Girlfriends are often so focused on what *they're* feeling, thinking, and needing that they don't realize they would be better served if they gave more thought as to how the *other* person is feeling, thinking, and needing. Put yourself in the other person's place, and you'll find your answers there.

- While communicating, try to imagine that you are observing the communication exchange from the outside, as a neutral third party. This will enable you to keep the emotion out of the process and truly find some understanding and solution for whatever is being discussed. This is a skill that can be learned in life, and it can boost your success in your personal as well as professional life.

- Remember that as far as communication is concerned, less is often more. The less you say and the more concisely and succinctly you say it, the easier it is to understand. Some girlfriends run into the habit of feeling that they need to keep talking to be heard. Nothing could be further from the truth!

Work on being a better listener in your life with the people that truly matter to you. Most of us make judgments about what is being shared even before the person talking has finished their thought. Truly listen!

Give it a Little More Thought, Girlfriend

1. On a scale of one to ten, how would you rate yourself as a communicator? Where do you feel there's room for improvement?

_____

_____

_____

_____

_____

2. Name a situation or event when the ability to intently listen could have made an important difference in your life.

_____

_____

_____

_____

_____

_____

3. At the present moment, do you struggle to be an effective communicator with anyone in your life? Why?

_____

_____

_____

_____

_____

_____

Your Call to Action

Recall a past communication experience that didn't end on a positive note. On paper, list all the reasons that may have contributed to that negative communication experience. What could you have done differently in the communication process that might have changed the outcome? Who was responsible for the breakdown— you, the receiver, or both of you?

_____

_____

_____

_____

_____

_____

Don't Be Afraid to do Battle!

When I was dating my husband in college, he came home with me to visit my family. While he was downstairs in the family room watching TV with my father, my mother and I had a horrendous, loud argument upstairs, complete with screaming and slamming doors. The fight continued for quite a while and eventually ended with the two of us crying and hugging each other, both apologizing. I think I should mention at this point that this was not an unusual occurrence at our house.

Downstairs, my then-boyfriend was agitated and upset. He heard what was going on upstairs and didn't know whether he should intervene or continue to act like nothing was happening. Finally, he couldn't take it anymore. He said to my father, "Aren't you going to do something about that?" and pointed to what was transpiring upstairs. My dad put down his newspaper, looked at him, and asked, "About what?" My boyfriend looked at my dad incredulously and said, "What's going on upstairs? It sounds horrible!" My dad nonchalantly replied, "Oh *that*? Don't worry. It'll be over soon." My dad didn't even hear it anymore because he knew it was the way we worked things out in our family.

So what's the point of this little memoir? Simple: our childhood shapes how we perceive and handle conflict in our lives. I grew up in an ethnic family in which we were encouraged to share our feelings, be they anger, sadness, disappointment, or any other emotions. I knew it was safe to share my feelings because we always hugged and apologized to each other at the conclusion of every fight. There was always closure to every episode and once it was over, it was truly over. My boyfriend, on the other hand, came from a home in which they did not verbally express their feelings in such a loud, explosive way. It was all new to him, so I imagine it was quite terrifying to witness for the first time!

If you grew up in a household where conflict was something to fear or avoid at all costs, this will surely affect how you handle conflict today. There is no way around it; at some point in your personal or professional life, you will be involved in a conflict situation. Being able to handle and resolve conflict is an important skill to master in order to have healthy relationships with co-workers, family, and friends.

Tips to Healthy Conflict Resolution:

Try to imagine what the other person in the conflict is feeling.

I know what you're thinking: When you're in the heat of the moment, it is difficult to focus on what the other person is thinking and feeling. You're so consumed with your own emotions that it's almost impossible to be empathetic toward the other individual and *truly listen*. However, if you can push yourself to try to understand their motivations, emotions, and perceptions in the situation, it will hopefully encourage both of you to arrive at a healthy understanding and compromise.

Be sure to clearly articulate what you need and want from the person.

Sometimes, we think it is very clear to everyone what we want because it is clear to us! But remember, everyone comes from a place of different perceptions, experiences, and emotions. The truth is that we don't always clearly state what we need to amend the situation and help us feel better. If you feel the other person should be able to figure out what you want, then YOU are standing in the way of a healthy resolution. Be assertive and state what you need!

Do your best to avoid being defensive during the conflict.

If you approach the conflict by following each statement made by the other party with one of your best comebacks, you will not move forward in the conflict. I understand that it's human nature to respond in this manner, but when you do, you will fail to address the real issue. This can be a problem for you if you were raised in a household in which you constantly felt like you were being attacked in some way. You need to attempt to really hear where the other person is coming from and respond in an objective manner, devoid of emotion. If you respond with defensive statements, believe me when I tell you that you will only escalate the situation.

State your feelings and needs clearly in "I" messages.

In other words, state what YOU are feeling and what YOU need to change without including the actions of the other person in the conflict. For example, "I feel hurt, disappointed, and unimportant when my birthday is forgotten." In this statement, your feelings are conveyed without a direct attack on the other person involved in the conflict. Therefore, there is more of a chance for understanding and problem-solving.

Reaffirm what the other party is stating in the interaction.

Often we don't truly hear what the other person is trying to say to us because we're focused on what we plan to say next. The bottom line is this: Everyone wants to be understood and truly heard in a relationship. If you are able to objectively listen to the other person involved in the conflict and restate what they are trying to say to you, you can begin to build the foundation for a resolution to the conflict.

Remember that the conflict is between the two of you, not the ghosts from your past!

Whenever you have an altercation with someone, you will bring your past experiences with you, good and bad. Keep the situation in check by not bringing your many emotions from past experiences into the relationship. Chances are that the individual in your conflict has a different set of values, emotions, and perceptions than your past ghost does. It's unfair to judge that they will respond to you in the same manner.

There is a difference between being assertive and aggressive!

A woman who is *aggressive* expresses her feelings and advocates for herself in an abusive, attacking manner. On the other hand, a woman who is *assertive* clearly and firmly states her opinions and feelings while advocating for her own rights. She does this in a manner that is neither dominating nor abusive. Be sure you understand the difference. Often, women struggle with exhibiting assertive behavior because they feel it is "mean" or "negative." On the contrary, an assertive woman will make it clear to the other individual that she has rights and boundaries of her own.

Being aggressive in a conflict situation can escalate the misunderstandings. Women with inner sass are assertive, positive, and committed to making a change for the better.

Give it a Little More Thought, Girlfriend

1. What was the conflict style in your home when you were growing up?

_____

_____

_____

_____

_____

_____

2. How does your childhood home life impact your conflict skills in your life today?

_____

_____

_____

_____

_____

_____

3. How do you usually handle conflict situations in your life?

_____

_____

_____

_____

_____

_____

4. In what ways would you like to improve your conflict resolution skills?

_____

_____

_____

_____

_____

_____

Your Call to Action

Think of a time when you were involved with a conflict that ended poorly. Now, using clear "I" messages, write down what would've been a more appropriate, effective way for you to share your feelings during the conflict. How would this approach have changed the outcome?

_____

_____

_____

_____

_____

_____

Is Multitasking a Girl's Best Friend?

Are you a serial multitasker? If so, heed my warning and pay attention to my story.

Monday was an incredibly busy day for me. I had a full day planned, running from one appointment to another. Even though I was helplessly tied up on the phone for most of the morning, I still attempted to develop my workshop and write a blog, all at the same time. At the very last minute, I ran upstairs, washed my hair, and threw on some clothes so I could make it to my appointments in time. Did I mention that I was also prepping part of our dinner so I wouldn't be too rushed in the evening? I ran to my car and sighed deeply when I was finally sitting inside it. Even with all that rushing around, I was still barely on time. Then, I looked down at my feet and realized something awful: I wasn't wearing any shoes! I felt ridiculous as I looked down at my bare socks. All I can say to you is this, girlfriends: I'm very relieved that I discovered my naked feet before I left the house. It would have been difficult to walk into a restaurant, where they frown upon serving those without shirts or shoes.

The point is: Maybe multitasking doesn't work as well as we think. Was I creating the absolute best workshop, or was I missing some important details? Was I truly penning a well-written blog? Did I put the right ingredients in the slow cooker, especially since I've been known to misread the measuring of ingredients when I talk to someone on the phone? The obvious answer to all these questions is a resounding "NO!"

Women seem to feel it's imperative that they are capable multitaskers in life. I've come across many women who are quite proud of this ability, but the truth is, when you're doing two or three things at once, you can't focus your attention on doing any one of them *really* well. Something has to give in the process. In my case, it was everything I was working on that day, including remembering to put on my footwear.

Research has proven that contrary to popular belief, humans can't do two things at once without the work quality suffering. They say women can't focus on more than one task at a time. *So*, girlfriends, it is virtually impossible for our brains to process the information on two competing tasks at the very same time. What we can do, however, is jump from one task to the next very quickly.

Sometimes, it seems as if we are moving way too fast in the world. Yes, it is great to be busy, active, and fully engaged in life. After all, every girlfriend wants to live a life full of passion, excitement, and adventure. However, there is such a thing as moving too fast and trying to accomplish more than is humanly possible. When we do this, we miss out on the ability to give our very best effort to each task and project we take on. When we're in such a hurry, we often miss the most important moments in life. So, slow down, take your time, and check your feet when you leave the house for the day!

Girls, have you ever noticed the need we have to do ten things at once? Do we do any of them well? Try blocking out time in your life to do one thing at a time and to be truly present and mindful of what you are doing.

Give it a Little More Thought, Girlfriend

1. Are you a serial multitasker? When do you multitask?

_____

_____

_____

_____

_____

_____

2. How has multitasking impacted your life in a negative way?

_____

_____

_____

_____

_____

3. Do you feel you live your life with mindfulness? When are you able to be fully present?

_____

_____

_____

_____

_____

_____

Your Call to Action

On a piece of paper, take an inventory of your daily life. Write down all the ways that you multitask during a typical day. Now, take a look at your list and decide how you can eliminate at least one multitasking experience a day. After one week, attempt to eliminate one more multitasking experience, another one the next week, and so on. Keep a journal of your daily successes and how these changes impact your life.

_____

_____

_____

_____

_____

_____

Stress-Busting for the Sassy Girlfriend

If I had a dollar for every time a woman told me she was stressed, I'd be a very wealthy woman! It's no wonder I hear this so often, as it's the norm in today's world for a woman's schedule to be extremely busy, running from one commitment to the next. Often, a woman serves the needs of everyone around her but neglects her own. She can be a giving friend, wonderful daughter, good worker, great wife, and an awesome mother, but problems arise when she stops listening to the signs from her own body that her life is on overload.

So what's a girlfriend to do? It's not realistic to think you can just jump ship and stop your life or abandon your responsibilities. However, you an adjust the way you approach life, which will make you feel less out of control.

Don't view the world in terms of black or white.

What do I mean by that? When you see life in rigid terms, you constantly feel as if your life isn't measuring up. For example, a woman who feels her house must be perfectly clean twenty-four hours a day when she already works full time and has three sports-committed kids is going to be stressed. If she were to adjust her thinking and be objective about the situation, she would be able to see how that immaculate home is not a realistic goal, nor does it reflect on her abilities as a mom or how successful she is in her life.

Instead of what is missing in life, focus on what you do have.

You can spend a horrendous amount of time focusing on what you don't have in life. Trust me, I've seen plenty of women who do this very well! At the end of the time spent lamenting your lot in life, I guarantee that you will not feel any better. In fact, you'll likely feel much, much worse. What if you took that valuable time and focused on what you're grateful for in life, on all the gifts that you *do* have? What if you lived your life in such a grateful way daily? I guarantee that this way of thinking will change your life and lower your stress level.

Stop carrying so many suitcases!

We've mentioned baggage and past ghosts quite a bit in this book, but that's because it begs repeating. The baggage you carry around from your past experiences will definitely increase your stress level! It's possible that you aren't even conscious of the fact that these past events are having such a huge impact on your present life. You might believe they are in the past and you don't want to stir up anything now, but the reality is that they are there, bubbling beneath the surface and affecting your body physically and emotionally. Sweeping things under the rug just makes for a bumpy rug! Do yourself a favor and get professional help. You'll be surprised how much better you'll feel.

Stop trying to prove that you're superwoman and can do it all because no one can.

Let me share something with you right now: LEARN TO SAY "NO!!" You can't do it all and do it well. This should be your new mantra. In order to live a healthy life, *have boundaries in your relationships* and know when you're taking on too much to handle. Listen to your body and see what it is trying to tell you. If you really listen, it's probably saying "Enough already!" I've met plenty of women who simply refuse to listen. Search for balance in your life. Sure, there will be times when your life is off kilter; just try to make it a short-term upheaval. Be aware of this imbalance and strive to get back on track. Listen to your instincts, girlfriend.

Stop worrying and stressing about events that haven't even happened yet.

Let me be honest here: I'm guilty of this very sin! I've spent time worrying and stressing about things that never came to fruition. Now that I look back, it all seems so silly and a big waste of time. Worrying and stressing isn't a very productive approach to problem-solving. Chances are, the very thing you're worried about probably won't even happen, so find something better to do with your time.

What can you do when you're feeling out of control and stressed? There are positive strategies you can use to decrease the stress-related symptoms you're experiencing.

Take a walk outside in nature.

Did you know that being outside in nature reduces your stress level? Research has shown that being outdoors helps to lower our blood pressure and calm our breathing. I often force myself to take a walk outside when I'm feeling stressed, and the fresh air works every time!

Listen to music.

Do you listen to music that makes you feel good about life? Be sure to have some go-to calming music that you can listen to when you're feeling stressed. Music has been proven to affect our moods and emotions, and the right kind of soothing music will make you feel calmer and better.

Get some exercise.

I can't mention this one enough: Daily exercise needs to be a way of life for every girlfriend. After taking part in an activity, I can think clearer, and I don't feel so overwhelmed. Every problem shrinks in size after a good workout—and your jeans size might too!

Talk with a friend.

Where would we be without our friendships? We need friends who can share our joy in the good times and support us through the bad times. Be careful with this suggestion, though, because the wrong friend can make you feel worse! Pick a supportive, nonjudgmental girlfriend who will truly listen and validate your feelings.

Learn how to meditate.

A number of my clients swear by this stress-dissolving

tactic and claim they cannot live without it. Many find yoga, accompanied by meditation, to be very effective for stress management, as well as other health benefits.

Get a massage.

If you are truly stressed, a massage can help relax your tightened muscles. In addition, it just feels great! The power of touch has been scientifically proven to decrease stress levels.

Take a bubble bath.

I take a hot bath at the end of every day. This signals to my body and mind that the hectic day is over so I can finally relax. When I get out of the bathtub, I immediately feel relaxed and am no longer stressed. It works every single time!

Find a hobby that makes you happy.

Whatever it is, make time in your life for the activities you enjoy. Do you feel passionate about jewelry-making, reading, knitting, or biking? Whatever it is that brings you joy and decreases your stress level, be sure to make time for it in your daily or weekly schedule.

Are you using any negative coping strategies to deal with your stress? These would include drinking, smoking, drugs, sex, gambling, food, and many more. If any of these are an issue for you, I encourage you to seek professional help.

If you are feeling stressed and overwhelmed, take an honest inventory of your life and make some changes. Stress takes a terrible toll on your body, not to mention your relationships. Change your life today, girlfriend!

If you find a lot of "should haves," "could haves," and "if onlys" in your conversations, then you need to change your way of thinking. You have nothing to gain by indulging in this type of thinking. Girlfriend, accept the past. You can't change it, but you can learn from it. Take that knowledge and keep moving forward!

Give it a Little More Thought, Girlfriend

1. Are you feeling stressed in any part of your life? What do you think is contributing to your feelings of stress?

_____

_____

_____

_____

_____

_____

Your Call to Action

Have a trusted friend help you take inventory of your life stressors and then develop a plan for decreasing them. Write down the strategies you will implement to handle the everyday stress that accompanies a busy lifestyle. Keep a journal of your daily progress.

_____

_____

_____

_____

Finding Your Inner "Integrity"

A couple years ago, I had a conversation with a mom whose daughter was in her senior year of high school. Like most moms, she wanted the absolute best for her child. Her daughter was extremely bright and had a brilliant future ahead of her, beginning with attending one of the top universities in the country. However, Mom shared with me that her daughter and her daughter's friend had been caught cheating on an exam in an advanced class in school. The teacher had no choice but to expel her from the class, in keeping with the school disciplinary policy for such an infraction, and the student's mother was extremely upset. The young woman's parents were livid with the school decision to expel their brilliant daughter from the class, and they caused quite a ruckus, going to the extent of threatening a lawsuit if the school followed through with the expulsion. As the mom explained the story to me, she shared that she thought it was horrible that the administrators at the school wanted to "ruin" the life of their daughter. She knew her daughter would lose her spot at the university if she was accused and punished for cheating. Never during the whole conversation did she indicate that she felt any disappointment or anger over her daughter's behavior.

I know what you're thinking, girlfriend, and I thought the same thing at the time. How interesting it is that her anger was directed only at the school officials and that she allowed her daughter to take no responsibility for her own actions! What did her daughter learn from her mother? I believe she learned that winning trumps all; apparently integrity did not play into the equation for them.

I am a firm believer in leading a life with integrity and character. In our world today, it's easy to get carried away with winning as opposed to doing the right thing. Success is often identified by going to the best college, getting the top job, and having the biggest home, the best car, or the largest bank account. Don't get me wrong: You should be commended if you've worked hard and earned these luxuries and positions, and you have a right to enjoy the fruits of your labors. However, if you need to sacrifice your integrity to "win" or earn the prize, it's simply not worth it.

So, what does it look like if a girlfriend has integrity?

A girlfriend with integrity has her own goals in life and aspires to achieve her dreams. However, she doesn't step on other people to get where she wants to go. She accomplishes her goals on her own terms without using people to get there.

A girlfriend with integrity respects another woman's relationship with a man. She does not expend any energy pursuing a man who is already taken and considers him off limits. Why? First, because a girlfriend with integrity and inner sass does not want a man that she will have to share; she knows she deserves much, much better. Second, a girlfriend with integrity would never treat another woman with such little respect, no matter who she is! Frankly, that's breaking the girlfriend code!

A girlfriend with integrity does not accept a job or continue working for a company if it requires her to violate her own code of ethics. Her integrity is her own moral code, made up of her deep beliefs. If she feels that who she is at the core is being compromised drastically, especially on a daily basis, she will make adjustments or reassess her goals in life.

A girlfriend with integrity treats ALL people with respect and dignity. Individuals do not impress her just because they have power, social standing, or financial status. Each person in her life is treated with respect until they show her they should be treated otherwise.

A girlfriend with integrity is a role models for her children and represents the person she desires for them to become in life. She doesn't believe in "Do as I say, not as I do." She lives her life true to who she is and is not swayed away from her own code of ethics. She is fully aware that hers and her partner's behavior directly molds the character of her children, so the two of them live this daily. Raising children with integrity is one of the most important goals for her as a mother.

A girlfriend with integrity passionately supports other women. This is one of the most important goals in her life. She does not compete with other women—end of story! She is secure and independent and knows who she is and what she wants out of life. She makes it her personal mission to encourage other women to find their inner sass. A girlfriend with integrity is confident and is not threatened by other women, so she wants all women to live their dream life!

A girlfriend with integrity is a great friend to have. She is there for you when life hits rough waters, and she will share in your big successes. She is honest and sincere and would never intentionally hurt you for her own emotional gain.

All too often, we accept others' definitions of who we are. Stop this!! Get some attitude and sass and remember who you are because you define YOU!!

Give it a Little More Thought, Girlfriend

1. Can you think of a time in your life when your integrity was threatened? What would you do differently today?

_____

_____

_____

_____

_____

_____

2. Is there someone close to you who struggles with doing the right thing? Does this affect your own life negatively?

_____

_____

_____

_____

_____

_____

Your Call to Action

Write about a specific experience when you were able to display your integrity in a situation. Be sure to include all the feelings and emotions you experienced during this time in life. Also, list the positive and negative outcomes from the situation.

_____

_____

_____

_____

_____

_____

Laughter Is the Best Medicine

When I was much, much younger and still dating, I refused to go out with anyone unless he could make me laugh. I believe I have a good sense of humor, and I was looking for someone who could match it. I grew up in a home filled with laughter and fun, and I wanted to re-create this feeling in my relationship.

During my thirty years of marriage, laughter has dampened the intensity of many-a-fight. Don't you hate it when someone says something funny to you while you're trying your hardest to stay angry? Frankly, it's impossible! The humor really puts everything into perspective. Come on! Is it really that devastating that the sink is full of dirty glasses AGAIN? In fact, I can honestly say I question whether our marriage would have lasted this long if we hadn't found the ability to laugh with/at each other. If you want to know what laughter can do for you, read on.

Laughter releases physical tension and stress.

Chances are, you're feeling some stress in your busy life. Make it a point to get together with a good friend and enjoy some deep belly laughs. Laughter relaxes all the muscles in your body and makes your stress melt away. It's impossible to feel anxious or sad when you're having a good laugh.

Laughter shifts your perspective when you're upset.

Imagine you're very upset with your teenage daughter. You've been thinking about the "incident" for the last two hours, and the more you think about it, the angrier you get. You discuss the issue with your friend, and she sees the humor in the situation. After a great laugh, you realize that maybe things aren't as bad as you initially thought. Somehow, after your laugh, things just seem better, and there now appears to be some hope for the situation. Laughter can do that for you.

Laughter attracts others to us.

Would you rather spend some time on a weeknight with

someone serious who doesn't crack a smile, or would you rather be with someone who makes you laugh like crazy? Be honest! It's not just *my* preference; most people are attracted to others who are happy and positive and make us laugh. It only makes sense that we want to be around people who make us feel good.

Laughter causes your body to release endorphins.

When we laugh, our bodies automatically release hormones called endorphins. These hormones cause a reaction that makes us feel good. Another side effect of this hormone release is relief from pain. Whether pain is physical or emotional, a good, hearty laugh can be great natural medicine.

Laughter enables us to express how we truly are feeling.

Let's say you have a fight with your husband and things are escalating. He comes back with a comment that you can't help but laugh at, as hard as you try to hold back. The two of you then burst out laughing, and the tension is broken! After the good laugh together, you're better able to express your true feelings to him, and you both better understand what the fight was really about. This, in turn, strengthens your relationship.

I can't tell you how many times laughter has helped me navigate an uncomfortable situation at work. Let's say you're in a meeting and tensions start to flare between two colleagues. Finding something humorous to add in the heat of the moment can really defuse the situation. I've found that humor and laughter are wonderful tools in such stressful situations.

Years ago, my seventh-grade son was in the kitchen with his two friends, and one friend began harassing the other. I was just on the verge of intervening when I heard my son interrupt them both by trying to make them laugh! He defused the moment, and they quickly went on to something else.

Laughter is key to you finding your inner sass. It is key to finding happiness in your relationships and navigating life's twists and turns. Finding the humor in everyday stressful situations will support you in your quest to be physically and emotionally healthy.

Did you know that belly laughs actually improve your body functioning? It's true! Not only is it fun, but it's good for your health!

Give it a Little More Thought, Girlfriend

1. Think about an experience from your past when laughter helped you change your perspective.

_____

_____

_____

_____

_____

_____

2. How can you incorporate more laughter into your life?

_____

_____

_____

_____

_____

_____

Your Call to Action

Call a friend or friends you can count on for some good laughter. Rent a funny movie and have a good time! Give yourself permission to let go of everything and just enjoy!

_____

_____

_____

_____

_____

Sisterhood Support

I really hate to do this, but I must reveal a dirty little secret about women. I believe we need to get this out in the open so we can deal with it. I've witnessed a number of experiences in which women were not supportive of each other. Not only were they not supportive, but they were also downright unkind. To be honest, in many of those experiences, the girlfriends used a passive-aggressive strategy to undermine their "competition."

So why do women act this way? Many times, women feel insecure and threatened by other women. Maybe this is a learned strategy from their childhood. Instead of recognizing and accepting this inferior feeling and finding a way to deal with it, they project these feelings onto other women. Now, I'm not saying you need to be besties with every woman that comes along, as that is not very realistic. As we've discussed in other parts of the book, you need to surround yourself with people who make you a better person. What I'm hoping is that you'll make it part of your life mission to support your sisterhood. As you accomplish your goals, make a pact to support and encourage other women whom you come across in your professional and personal life.

Many years ago, I was working in a position where I was able to utilize a number of my talents and expand a program. I was successful in accomplishing my goals, but I hit a low point in the job when I became very unhappy and unfulfilled. Every morning, I rationalized that I was doing the right thing by staying on the job. I had grown close to one of my bosses, and I respected her immensely. Feeling discouraged and frustrated, I decided to call a meeting with her to ask for guidance.

After listening to me pour my heart out, she interrupted and asked, "What do you want to do with your life?" I had no idea what she was talking about, because I was in the middle of telling her about my unhappiness at the present job; her question threw me. I didn't answer, so she asked again. She wanted to guide me away from unproductive complaining and get me to take action. Out of nowhere, came my thought: "I want to go back to school and become a mental health therapist." We were both shocked by that statement because until that moment, I had never articulated it to anyone. She responded like a Nike commercial: "Then just do it!"

What followed was a five-minute diatribe from me as to why that would be impossible, including the "fact" that I was not smart enough to make it through school. She recognized the fear that had taken hold of me and spent the next ten minutes reminding me of everything I had achieved in my life. She added that she thought I was one of the smartest people she knew. By the end of her pep talk, she had given me enough confidence to entertain the notion that I really could accomplish that seemingly impossible goal.

But it didn't end there, girlfriends. Sitting beside me, she looked at different courses online and encouraged me to call the university department and make an appointment to gather more information. She then insisted that the two of us go to campus together for my appointment. And the rest is history.

The bottom line? None of that was in her job description! In fact, she could have easily encouraged me to stay on the job, which would have made her life much easier, but she didn't. She believed in supporting women to achieve their dreams, and she did everything she could to help others. She paid it forward on a regular basis.

How lucky I was to have her in my life! She helped me see how important it was to have the support of another woman who believes in you. At the time, I needed a strong, successful woman to help me see that I could dream. I needed the extra push to take that jump!

So, girlfriends, make it your mission to support your sisters. Encourage them to accomplish their goals, try new experiences, and be their best selves. Encourage their inner sass!

Girlfriends, we need to support each other on a daily basis. Today, be mindful of letting at least one woman know how much you appreciate her. Today, tell another woman what makes her great. You will truly make her day, and she'll hopefully pay it forward!

Give it a Little More Thought, Girlfriend

1. Can you think of a time in your life when a girlfriend pushed you forward and encouraged you to dream? What happened?

_____

_____

_____

_____

_____

2. Be honest: Are you a support sister for other women? When have you encouraged or supported someone else?

_____

_____

_____

_____

_____

Your Call to Action

Is there a woman you know who needs some support to accomplish her goals? She doesn't necessarily have to be a good friend—just a girlfriend who's in need of some guidance and support in order for her to move forward in life. This one unselfish act can forever change another sister's life, so get out there and pay it forward.

_____

_____

_____

_____

_____

_____

The Girlfriend Code

I've worked with many women in the past who struggle with having solid friendships in their lives; it's difficult for them to maintain good, healthy friendships over a long period of time. This is often because they don't understand what it really takes to be a good friend. Sometimes they don't realize there are unwritten rules that friends need to follow.

I remember making plans with my good friends to go bridesmaids' dress shopping for my wedding. We worked out a date that all three of us had free. As the day approached, I became more and more excited to share that time with people who were so important to me. Two hours before we were supposed to meet, my close friend called to tell me she had to cancel because her boyfriend had secured tickets to a high school basketball game that was about to start. When I expressed my hurt and disappointment, she became angry with me and said I was making a big deal out of the situation.

Our friendship never recovered from that one experience. As time went on, she made it clear that she didn't feel she had done anything wrong. On top of that, she was angry that I had any expectations of her in our friendship. I struggled with whether or not I should continue to nurture a friendship with someone who wouldn't even validate my feelings. We both knew her boyfriend had encouraged her to break the plans, but the real truth was that she broke one of those certain special rules that true girlfriends live by! I call it the **Girlfriend Code.**

Never break plans with a good girlfriend to be with a guy

Do you hear that, girlfriends? Guys come and go, but we need to cherish our good girlfriends. Whether you are going to a movie, just hanging out together, or going to try on bridesmaids' dresses, breaking plans is a big no-no. Not only is it hurtful, but it also expresses how little you value your friendship and sends a clear message to the guy that you will drop everything for him! That is not a healthy way to live your life!

Never pursue a guy who is already taken.

I don't care if the two of you are just perfect for each other; a guy who is already in a relationship is off limits. As long as a guy is involved with another woman, he is not available—end of story! Even if the guy is involved with a girl you are not friends with, you would still be violating the girlfriend code. This is where integrity and self-worth come into the picture!

Never compete with a girlfriend.

Contrary to what you see on *Real Housewives*, true girlfriends don't compete; they support each other. When you feel the need to compete with other women, you are sending a clear message that you are threatened and feel insecure. Strong, accomplished women with high self-esteem feel no need to overtly compete with other women. This goes for girlfriends who feel the desire to compete vicariously through their children's many accomplishments. The next time you feel the urge to brag, take a good look inside.

Don't engage in gossip about your girlfriend with other girlfriends.

When the talk turns to your good friend who is absent, do the right thing and defend her. It is easy to talk negatively about someone who is not present. Take into account that next time, it could be you whom they are talking about.

I have said this before, and I will say it again: We need our girlfriends in our lives! Cherish your relationships and try your best to live by the **GIRLFRIEND CODE!**

The definition of a great girlfriend: She helps celebrate your happiness when things are going well and supports you when it feels as if the world is crashing down on you! She shares the ride of life with you!

Give it a Little More Thought, Girlfriend

1. Have you ever broken the girlfriend code? How did it make you feel?

_____

_____

_____

_____

_____

_____

2. How could you have handled the situation differently?

_____

_____

_____

_____

_____

_____

3. Is there anything you would add to the girlfriend code?

_____

_____

_____

_____

_____

Your Call to Action

Write about a time when you honored the girlfriend code and did the right thing for another girlfriend. How did it make you feel? Be sure to include the repercussions from making this decision and the accompanying feelings and emotions.

_____

_____

_____

_____

_____

Be a Mom with Inner Sass

I can honestly say that the role of mom is probably one of the most difficult, yet rewarding jobs that exists in the market today. I bet all moms would agree that every other job they've worked in pales in comparison to this role. One day you're on top of the world, feeling like the best mom who's ever lived, and the next day, you might be wondering whether you're fit to take on this responsibility! Let's face it: There are a lot of ups and downs, stresses and struggles. How do you get through this rollercoaster ride with your sanity intact? Read on, girlfriend.

Try to keep a good perspective on the situation.

I was shopping for groceries the other day, and I heard an adorable little five-year-old girl tell her mother she found another coupon for her. Apparently, she'd discovered that she could pull the coupons from the display and was proud of her new ability, but Mom responded harshly and loudly that she would be in timeout if she did it one more time. Really? I totally support parents who teach their children to act properly in public places, but this just seemed extreme. Save the timeout for a situation that truly calls for it, as I'm sure there will be plenty to choose from. Keep your perspective on what really matters and when it's the right time to have a good laugh and just let it go.

Don't get caught up in your child's life.

Every child is going to experience hurts and disappointments as they grow up. Eventually, he or she is going to come home one day and tell you that little Miles said he doesn't want to be his friend. Your child is going to be hurt and so are you. You need to keep in mind that everyone has this experience at least once while growing up. Your child needs to learn how to cope with rejection so he or she can handle it adequately later in life. As we know, it happens to everyone! Be very wary about getting involved in these types of situations. Empower your son or daughter to handle their own issues, starting at a young age, when appropriate. The more you step in, the less they feel confident that they can take care of their own needs. Make it a goal that your child be self-reliant.

Let your child be who they're meant to be.

One of the most important things you can do for your child is to help them discover who they are and what they need in life to be happy. Sometimes, this is difficult for parents because of their preconceived vision of what their child SHOULD be. For example, I had a client who refused to believe her child was not the stellar athlete she expected him to be in life. This put stress on their relationship and negatively impacted the child's self-esteem. Accept your child for who they are, not for who you desire them to be. This is no small feat for a parent and takes patience and hard work.

Don't try to be your child's friend: Be their MOM.

I've worked with women who believe their kids are more than just their kids; they're their best friends. Typically, I see this with women who have had unhappy childhoods and poor relationships with their own parents. In their desire to have a relationship very different from their own, they form a relationship with their child that lacks healthy boundaries. Often, this happens in situations where the mom expects her children to serve her own emotional needs. Her children become her confidantes, privy to information that's way beyond their scope of emotional maturity. Kids need rules to feel safe, and they do best when they know that someone is in control.

If you want your child to have character and integrity, be a good role model.

It starts with you, Mom—no two ways about it! You want your kid to be kind and carry him- or herself with integrity? Then you need to live it daily. They learn this directly from YOU! If you don't want your child to take shortcuts in life, then you need to watch your own behavior. If you want your kid to value honesty and fairness over always winning, you need to live that behavior. If you want your child to value being an individual and unique over fitting in, then you need to model that daily. Last, if you truly want your child to be kind to others, practice this in your life.

Be your own person and never lose track of YOU.

Being a mom is an all-consuming role, and it's easy to lose track of that person at the core! Suddenly, your days are filled with running around and serving the needs of everyone but YOU. Be sure to save some time to pursue your own dreams and hobbies. You'll be very busy, but that doesn't mean you can't make it a priority to carve out time to take care of you and do some of the things you love. In turn, you will be able to be a better mom to your children. On top of that, it's important for your kids to see that you value YOU!

Listen to your kids.

The key to being an exceptional mom is to be a good listener. If you know how to listen, you will understand your child better and eliminate a number of stressful situations. Look beneath the surface and see what they are really trying to say to you. This becomes even more important as children become teenagers and begin to pull away from their moms. Often, we are so involved in our own emotional reaction to the situation that we miss the true meaning of the message being sent by our child. Try to get outside your own head and listen to what your son or daughter is really saying to you.

Channel what it feels like to be your kid's age.

If more people were able to accomplish this, there would be less stress and more harmony in the world. What do I mean by this? Imagine that you have a teenage son going to his first dance with a girl. When you drop him off where the kids are gathering, he pleads with you to leave quickly. Anxious and stressed, he begs you not to stay with the other parents and take pictures. Actually, my own son would recognize this scenario well because he actually pleaded with me to leave his first formal dance. When this happened, my first reaction was disappointment and hurt, but my second thought was, "How did I feel at his age? Hmm...just like him!" I respected his request because I remembered what it felt like to be fifteen, and I got it! The good news is that as he became more confident, he loved having me around.

I hope each and every one of you becomes a mom who has found her inner sass. The work is tough, but it's so very worth it for you and your kids!

If you want your son or daughter to be a confident person with high self-esteem, look in the mirror. You need to model the life that you want him or her to have. They learn their self-worth by watching you!

Give it a Little More Thought, Girlfriend

1. How does your style as a parent differ from your own mother's parenting style? What have you improved upon and what still needs some work?

_____

_____

_____

_____

_____

2. Name five adjectives that describe each one of your children. Was it easy for you? If not, why?

_____

_____

_____

_____

_____

_____

3. Do you truly listen to your kids? Where is there room for improvement?

_____

_____

_____

_____

_____

_____

Your Call to Action

List the ways that you're able to take care of YOU as a woman while you take care of everyone else in the family. Include the ways that you're able to continue to grow as an individual, independent of being a mother.

_____

_____

_____

_____

_____

_____

The P Word

I once worked with a woman who desperately wanted to change her life. She was unhappy with her financial situation, her living arrangements, her educational achievements, and her relationship. Together, we worked out a detailed plan as to how she could move forward. Each week, she came back to see me and shared how much she had accomplished from the week before, which was not much at all. We assessed what she felt was impeding her progress to move forward, and then I sent her off to face the following week. The same pattern played out over and over because she was battling the P word: **procrastination!**

If you're a procrastinator, it didn't happen out of nowhere. You didn't inherit a gene that makes you susceptible to this behavior. Chances are, you learned this pattern back in your childhood, and it continues to be part of your life today. There are a few basic reasons why people procrastinate:

The work you need to get done is difficult and not that much fun.

Let's face it: Changing your life is hard work. If you want to lose fifty pounds, it's understandable that you would find it challenging because it's not fun to diet! I'm willing to bet we would all love to eat a juicy hamburger with fries instead of a piece of grilled fish with broccoli. It's human nature to want to feel good NOW! Working on a long-term goal is difficult because it doesn't provide the instant gratification that so many of us crave. It's so easy to tell yourself to enjoy now and go back on your diet tomorrow. The problem arises when tomorrow never comes.

You don't want the goal bad enough to change your behavior.

Some people procrastinate because they just don't want the change bad enough. For example, they might verbalize that they are certain they want to go back to school and finish their degree, yet they have trouble moving forward on any of their plans. They may decide they'll fill out the application on the weekend, but the weekend comes and goes, and they get nothing done. The truth is, if it's important enough to them and if they desperately want to change their life, they'll make it happen. I've seen this many times with past clients who try to move forward in life. Often, they need to hit rock bottom before they make the change in their life.

You are easily distracted from your goal.

I'll let you in on a secret: I'm easily distracted and have had to learn certain strategies to stay on track in my life. I've been known to start one project, get distracted, and end up working on something else entirely. If you struggle with ADD or ADHD behaviors, this might sound familiar. This can also be the cause of your procrastination tendencies. For example, maybe you make it a goal for the day to clean out your closet, but you get sidetracked while looking at your shoes in the back of the closet. This leads to you deciding that you need a new pair of red shoes to go with the outfit you just brought home from the store yesterday, so you forget about your closet-cleaning and take on a new mission of heading to the shoe store for just the right shade of red. In this way, goals never reach their finish because they are forgotten about in exchange for something else.

You are afraid you won't succeed at your goal.

For some people, working toward certain goals can be overwhelming and scary. The fear of failure can be so terrifying that it inhibits your ability to even get started. It becomes a self-fulfilling prophecy; you fear you will fail at the task, and that is exactly what happens since you never get started!

Fortunately, there are strategies you can use to combat procrastination:

Make a list of your goals daily, weekly, and monthly.

Make sure your goals are realistic and concrete and have dates of completion. Assess your progress daily and weekly and be sure to assess your progress on an ongoing basis.

Learn to talk back to the little voice in your head.

You know that voice—the one that convinces you that it's okay to have that second glass of wine and relax instead of finishing your proposal for work. In order to combat procrastination, you need to engage that voice in a conversation. The first step is to recognize when that voice is sabotaging your efforts to complete goals. Be aware that we all have a steady stream of background chatter in our heads; at times it is supportive, but at other times, it can be quite destructive and sabotaging. Learn to talk back to the voice and refuse to give in.

Eliminate your distractions.

I recently had a conversation about this with a girlfriend who had just started grad school. I encouraged her to go to the library to study to avoid the many enticing distractions in her home. She acknowledged that she would have difficulty studying at a coffee shop because she would end up people-watching and listening to conversations. Be honest and find what works for you. Let's face it: We're so good at finding distractions in life when we are working on something that isn't fun!

Find a friend who will hold you accountable to achieve your goals.

Let's pretend your goal is to start an exercise program at the gym and eat healthier. In the past, you ended up sleeping in every day. Enlist the help of a friend to check in with you and keep you on task. Having a partner with the same goals will increase your chances of succeeding.

The truth is that at some point in your life, you will wrestle with this issue. It is important to be honest with yourself. Head on, you must face whatever it is that's holding you back from accomplishing your goals and make a plan to change your ways.

It's so much easier to stay in DENIAL than it is to accept unpleasant things in your life. Acceptance takes hard work and forces us to feel some things that might be scary. Girls, get some sass and keep moving forward!

Give it a Little More Thought, Girlfriend

1. Is there a goal in your life that has been difficult for you to achieve due to procrastination?

_____

_____

_____

_____

_____

_____

2. After reviewing the reasons we procrastinate, why do you think you are struggling to achieve your desired goal?

_____

_____

_____

_____

_____

_____

3. What procrastination strategies do you think you would utilize next time?

_____

_____

_____

_____

_____

_____

Your Call to Action

Are you struggling with achieving one goal in particular? After reviewing the reasons you procrastinate, write down why you believe you are struggling to achieve that goal. Make a list of the procrastination strategies you can implement in this specific situation.

_____

_____

_____

_____

_____

_____

Get Moving, Girlfriend!

Did you make time in today's schedule to exercise? I hope so. I understand that it's impossible for you to add one more thing to your to-do list. I hear you, and we all know that life can be crazy. I have heard this many times before. But the reality of the situation is this: If you want to have strong inner sass, you HAVE to incorporate exercise into your everyday life. Why? Let's have a look.

Exercise improves your physical health.

Imagine that the elevator to your apartment is broken and you are forced to walk up eight flights of stairs. Is this going to be difficult for you? Do you have the stamina to do so without getting winded? If you have been getting aerobic exercise on a daily basis, you will be able to do this with ease. Other than giving us stamina to face whatever life throws at us, exercise also helps protect us against heart problems, circulatory issues, bone loss, and many more diseases that can affect us as we age. Have you ever noticed how people who exercise seem to stand a little straighter, walk with more confidence, and be more comfortable in their bodies? At my last check-up, my doctor was shocked at my low blood pressure, considering my age. I attribute this to my daily exercise and long bike rides up and down hills.

Exercise improves your mental health.

Do you know the number one intervention to alleviate depressive symptoms? Daily exercise! That's right, girlfriend: Exercise has been proven to be more effective than antidepressants and talk therapy. When I worked with women who were struggling with depression, I encouraged them to go for a walk with me. Every single time, they came back from the walk feeling better than when they first walked into my office. When you exercise, your body releases "feel-good" chemicals. Isn't that a great way to start every day? On top of that, when you push yourself to achieve goals in workouts, your self-esteem will skyrocket! Before I began cycling, I never thought I would be capable of biking for thirty miles with ease! I'm quite proud of myself!

Exercise keeps your weight down.

If you are interested in a weight loss regimen, exercise is a must. Watching what you eat, coupled with cardio exercise is the optimal way to bring your weight down. The more exercise you do, the more fuel your body burns; it's as simple as that. As you age, it's more and more difficult to build muscle; therefore, it's even more important to challenge yourself in workouts. The more muscle you have, the more fuel/fat you will burn!

Exercise helps you relieve stress and anxiety.

Exercise is a natural stress reducer. If I'm feeling stressed or anxious, I force myself to break away from what I'm doing and take a walk outside. Almost immediately, I feel my breathing slowing, and a feeling of calmness takes over my whole body. Whenever I had a spat with my teenage son, I always encouraged him to go for a run outside in the fresh air, and he always came back to the house with a clearer head and a calmer disposition.

Exercise helps you sleep better.

Everywhere I go, I hear girlfriends complaining about how they can't sleep at night. A couple months ago, I was at a party where eight women were sitting around the table talking. While one woman began to share her difficulties in getting a good night's sleep, each woman began to chime in about having the same problem. A couple of the ladies were even on medication for insomnia. I was the only one who had no trouble sleeping soundly through the night. I attribute my commitment to exercise as the number one reason for my good sleep.

Exercise should be fun.

Do you remember when you were young and you loved running outside and climbing trees or monkey bars? This was exercise for you, but you didn't even realize it at the time because you were just having fun. One of the main reasons we fail to keep up with our exercise regimens is because we become bored. Do you think exercise is about doing the same thing time and time again? You know what happens? You lose interest quickly because it's work. Exercise should be fun and enjoyable. Don't think of it as something you HAVE to do, but something you WANT to do. For example, if you love dancing, take dance classes. If you used to enjoy playing soccer, join a soccer group. There are so many different classes you can take and groups you can join. Channel your inner child and have fun!

We always have CHOICES in life. Sometimes, girlfriends try to paint a picture of things happening to them. Remember to take control of your own life and make things happen!

Give it a Little More Thought, Girlfriend

1. Do you feel you have a healthy exercise routine in your life? Why or why not?

_____

_____

_____

_____

_____

2. If you don't, what do you feel is holding you back?

_____

_____

_____

_____

_____

Your Call to Action

Develop an action plan for incorporating exercise in your daily life. Be sure to include reasonable goals that can be met daily, weekly, and monthly. Start out **slowly** and work your way to larger goals. Enlist the help of a friend for support. Keep a log of each day's accomplishments and your feelings after you've completed your daily goal.

_____

_____

_____

_____

_____

_____

Give to Others to Find Your Happiness

Oh yes, the elusive search for happiness. Many-a-book has been written to reveal the secrets to living happily ever after. Well, girlfriend, here's my advice on how you can get a jumpstart on happiness and live the good life: Give back to others. One of the keys to finding your best life is embracing the act of volunteering and caring about the world. Would you like to understand how giving to others can change your life? Then keep reading.

Giving to others makes you feel productive.

I had a client who was struggling with depression. She was unemployed and had way too much idle time on her hands. She was looking for a job, but in the meantime, the days seemed unbearably long. I encouraged her to volunteer her time at a nonprofit agency so she could have some sense of structure in her day. That one change in her life led to many more positive changes, and she began to have more reasons to get up in the morning because many people were counting on her to complete certain responsibilities.

Giving to others enables you to stop focusing too much on YOU!

Every girlfriend has at least one friend who focuses a bit too much on her own problems. You know the one. Every day brings another major crisis. Her speech is peppered with "If only..." and "It's not fair." She is so self-absorbed in her pain that she can't see outside the bubble she's created. Do you know what would help her? Taking the opportunity to focus on giving to others. This would enable her to take a timeout from her own pain and concentrate on more productive activities.

Giving to others enables you to develop new skills.

Let's say you just became unemployed, and of course, you're feeling down and disappointed. You can do one of two things: spend your days searching for a job and nothing else or give back in some capacity while you continue to look for a job. Now here's the kicker: It's possible that you can find your true calling in life while you are volunteering your time. It's also possible to uncover some hidden skills and talents that you have long forgotten while you've been working for pay. It's entirely possible that your volunteering can lead you in a totally different direction in your life! The point is, it's a win-win when you give back to others.

Giving to others gives you a reality check.

Maybe you're going through a bad time. If your life is a rollercoaster ride, you're on the lowest dip and wondering when you'll ever get to ride another hill. Nothing changes your down mood more than helping others who are worse off than you. All of a sudden, things aren't quite as bad. You feel the pain others are feeling and strangely, you feel grateful for what you *have* instead of what you *don't* have. It's funny how that works in life!

Giving to others gives you a social network.

Depending on your lifestyle, you can become isolated in your daily routine. For example, you might work for a small company where you come in contact with the same people every day. Maybe you work out of your house, like many people do today. It's great to talk to your boss in your pajamas, but sometimes you crave a bit more face-to-face interaction. As we all know, this can become quite mundane and downright boring. Breaking up your week by getting involved in a charitable organization can force you out into the universe again. You might come across some fabulous people whom you would've never met in your everyday business life.

Giving to others makes you feel good.

Experts say exercise releases hormones that make you feel good, and the same thing happens when you put caring about others into action. The feeling of helping others who are less fortunate is one that just can't be described. Somehow, you will end up receiving a much greater gift than the one you gave. Giving enables you to connect with the world and feel like a part of the universe. It helps you get a sense of community.

I feel it's important to give you a word of caution here: It is possible to take caring for others to an extreme. Life is about balance, about taking care of YOU while caring for others. Imbalance on either side is not a healthy way to live your life. Hyperfocusing too much on yourself will make you feel miserable and miserable to be around. Focusing on others' needs exclusively and ignoring your own can still make us miserable and miserable to be around. How so? Girlfriends who live their lives giving to others without nurturing themselves end up angry, bitter, and frustrated. Many become involved in codependent relationships. They become masters of martyrdom, exhausted and disconnected from their own needs. Be sure to find your sweet spot, your give-and-take balance, and hold on to your healthy boundaries.

Girlfriend, it's admirable to be a giver in life and feel passionate about taking care of others. Just make sure you balance this with taking care of you. Listen to your gut, and if you need a timeout, take it!

Give it a Little More Thought, Girlfriend

1. Do you give your time to others on a regular basis? How does it make you feel?

_____

_____

_____

_____

_____

2. Do you feel you have a balance in life between giving and taking? How could you improve your balance?

_____

_____

_____

_____

_____

Your Call to Action

On a piece of paper, make two columns. On one side, write down all the ways in which you volunteer your time to others during the year. On the other side, write all the ways in which you take care of YOU. Is there a reasonable balance? How can you make some changes so your life is more balanced?

_____

_____

_____

_____

_____

_____

All Work and No Play Makes You a Dull Girlfriend!

Are you working hard at becoming a success in your field? I applaud you and am impressed by your dedication and discipline. Do you work day and night to get ahead? Let's say you LOVE your work and have a passion for whatever it is that you do. Even then, you can still have too much of a good thing.

I LOVE what I do. It is my dream to empower women to move ahead in life and accomplish their goals. Nothing gives me greater joy than to see one of my clients find happiness and understanding of self. The truth is that I can work from the time I get up in the morning until the time I collapse into bed at night on new ideas, workshops, writing projects, and life plans for clients. However, a couple of weeks ago, something changed. I began to notice that I was feeling tired no matter how much I slept. Usually, I'm the person who can't stop moving. I was blessed with a lot of energy—maybe too much energy at times, but that seemed to be tapering off. I would sit down to write a blog, but nothing would come to me; whereas in the past, I would never have to search for ideas. I would plan to work on developing my workshop and I just couldn't focus. This was frustrating, and I didn't understand what had changed. And then it came to me: I was getting burned out. I had reached the point where I had eliminated everything else in my life except my business work. The more I eliminated, the more tired I felt and the less creative I became.

After giving this idea some thought, I realized that even when I was doing something other than business work, I was still thinking about business. From the time I got up in the morning until the moment I went to bed, I only thought about one thing: my business and my clients. Once I realized how unhealthy and counterproductive this was, I decided the best medicine for my "illness" was to turn on the television and watch an episode of

The Real Housewives of New Jersey. Now, you might think, "Wow! That's really trash TV. I can't believe she watches that." You're right, as it's not the most intelligent form of entertainment, but it was exactly what I needed. There's nothing better when you are mentally exhausted than to watch an episode of such a show, for it is a pure guilty pleasure. And that leads me to the point of this whole discussion: EVERYONE NEEDS DOWNTIME AWAY FROM WORK.

Whether you love your job or not, you need diversions in your life to keep you fresh and rested. Maybe watching trashy TV isn't what you need, but find something pleasurable to do that helps you unwind and let go, the key phrase being **let go.** Here are some ideas that will help you to become reenergized:

Read a book that's relaxing and helps you focus on something other than work. I have been guilty of reading self-improvement books, which don't exactly allow me to stop thinking about work! Don't fall into this trap! The best move I ever made was to join a book club. This forced me to read enjoyable books that I would have never chosen on my own.

Start a new hobby that's very different than anything else you're doing in your life. Trying new things gets the creative juices flowing again.

Take a walk outside in nature and clear your mind. Every time your mind goes back to thinking about work, redirect your thinking to something else.

Join a new club or organization that interests you and uses a very different skill set than you use daily at your workplace. You may feel as if you don't have the time to indulge in a new venture, but it is possible that this is exactly what you need.

Make time for exercise in your life. When I'm on the elliptical, I often get bursts of creativity. Exercise stimulates your brain, and it's also great for your physical health. I know you have heard this before, but exercise is the best medicine for burnout syndrome.

Put parameters around the hours you work. Make a schedule for yourself and be disciplined about scheduling in downtime. If you work from home, it is more difficult to let go of your work and responsibilities. Thanks to today's technology, you could potentially work twenty-four hours a day from home. This means you might revel in the fact you can work in your pajamas, but boundaries between work and relax time can become a bit blurred. That's why it's important to establish a firm designation between your work and play time—and stick to it!

Unplug from all your technology now and then. When you're taking some downtime, force yourself to turn off the computer, phone, etc. Frankly, we've all become quite addicted to the stimulation that our e-mail, text messaging, Facebooking and tweeting can bring to us. However, there are times when you need to force yourself to *just disconnect.*

We all need balance in our lives to stay healthy. Maybe it's not work that's burning you out: Maybe you're a stay-at-home mom who needs a break from being with the kids. Good moms know they need balance in their lives—time away from their kids so they can reconnect with their real self. Walking away for a few hours enables you to refresh so you can meet life's expectations with renewed energy and passion.

Do you take on too much and then complain about the amount? Reassess your life and where you want to invest your time. Be sure to take time for yourself.

Give it a Little More Thought, Girlfriend

1. Do you have problems letting go and allowing yourself to enjoy life?

_____

_____

_____

_____

_____

_____

2. Do you feel you lead a healthy, balanced lifestyle? What areas need improvement?

_____

_____

_____

_____

_____

_____

Your Call to Action

Write down your work schedule and all the responsibilities you have in your daily life. Now, review your schedule and find ways to add short breaks from work into your day. Be sure there are very firm boundaries during your day that separate your work life from the other parts of your life.

_____

_____

_____

_____

_____

_____

The Grass Isn't Always Greener

My first job after graduating from college was an assistant managing position in retail. The job market was horrible at that time, so I was lucky to have a job at all. I was earning barely enough to survive. I had just gotten married, and my husband still had two years of schooling ahead of him. Needless to say, money was tight—so *tight* that I remember searching the couch cushions one night so we could treat ourselves to a Frosty at the local Wendy's.

At the store, I worked with a girl who had gone to school with me at Ohio State. She had graduated with a degree in education, but that year, there were no teaching jobs available, so she worked as a sales clerk in the store that I managed. Her husband had received a plum job right out of college due to his connections as an Ohio State football player. I thought she was just beautiful, sophisticated, and had great style. I coveted her life: the clothes she wore, the fact that she worked just to keep busy, and the fact that she and her husband could easily afford all the Frosties they wanted because they were clearly not hurting for money.

After we got to know each other, she began to tell me stories, and I realized that her life was not as rosy as I had envisioned in my envy state. She explained to me that her previous boyfriend was also a former football player and was very well known and popular. Honestly, I could see that she was very impressed by that. Further into her story, I learned that he had physically abused her. Nevertheless, she stayed in that tumultuous relationship for quite a while before going on to date the man who became her husband. In essence, she had married her husband because he could take care of her.

That was my first experience with wild envy and the grass-is-always-greener misconception. There were a lot of "if onlys" in my thinking during that time: "If only I looked like her...

If only I lived like her, then everything would be different and better." After she shared more of her life, I realized that things were not as perfect as I had envisioned them to be. She had married her husband to be safe, something I would never do. She had allowed men to control and abuse her, something that would have never happened to me. I was a strong young woman, and back then I desired a career and to be financially and emotionally independent. That experience forced me to take a good look at myself and reflect on why I was comparing myself to others.

If you're guilty of the green-eyed monster, here are a couple of things you should think about:

You have nothing to gain by comparing your life to others.

Here's a news flash for you: There will always be someone who has a more perfect husband, a bigger house, a more expensive car, and smarter kids. Frankly, you can waste a lot of time in life coveting what belongs to others. The bottom line is that you might receive short-term happiness from material possessions, but it certainly doesn't get you through the long term. A material possession has a very short shelf life for making you happy. True and lasting happiness comes from within.

If you are envious of another woman, take a good look inside.

If that green-eyed monster is visiting you in life, it's time to do a good assessment of your life. Dig down deep and figure out where that unhappiness is coming from. Are you feeling unfulfilled in your job? Are you stuck in an unfulfilling or unhealthy relationship? Do you fear moving forward in life and are trapped by your fear? Do you feel inadequate as a person and need material things to fill you up? Face it: If you're trapped by envy, it's clear that you're not feeling good about you. Do some soul-searching and find the answers. You'll be glad you did.

Comparing yourself to another woman is an incredible waste of time.

It truly accomplishes nothing. All it does is make you feel worse than before you started! Be proactive. If you covet someone's figure, start on your own exercise program. If you're jealous of her relationship with her husband, work on YOUR relationship with your hubby. If you are jealous of her job, take a look at what you desire to do in life and change.

Learn to accept where you are right now.

Some girlfriends live their whole lives wishing they were someone else, somewhere else, or with someone else. I've worked with women who appear to have it all, yet they're still coveting others and miserable in life. On the other hand, I've met women who have very, very little yet are satisfied with their lot in life. It's all about learning to be happy right where you are at the moment. It's definitely not about searching for the next best thing to come along and fill you up. Instead, it's about being okay with you!

So, girlfriends, make sure the green-eyed monster stays far away. Do the hard work now so the only woman you desire to be is YOU!

Are you caught up in the emotion of envy? Stop focusing on what others possess and start working today on what you truly desire in life!

Give it a Little More Thought, Girlfriend

1. Have you been jealous of another woman at some point in your life? What did she possess that you desired?

_____

_____

_____

_____

_____

2. What do you think your envy truly reveals about you?

_____

_____

_____

_____

_____

Your Call to Action

Write about a time in your life when you were jealous of what another woman possessed. Include the feelings and emotions you experienced during that time and what you think was really lurking beneath the jealousy.

_____

_____

_____

_____

_____

_____

Rock What You've Got

Is it possible to get together with a group of women and *not* have a conversation that surrounds dieting? That is, the diet you're currently on, the one you're thinking about starting, or possibly the one you just quit because it didn't work? The point is, women are obsessed with their bodies and how they never quite stack up. When was the last time you heard a bunch of women discussing how much fun it was to go swimsuit shopping? I'm pretty sure that if we took a poll right now, it would reveal our strong distaste for trying on bathing suits in fluorescent lighting.

Where did this obsession with our body parts come from? I believe all women learn at a young age that there is a very narrow definition of female beauty. Also, we were and still are bombarded daily with messages that reinforce unrealistic expectations of women. In addition to this, our cultural admiration with youth does not help us accept our aging process.

So, how do we feel good about US when we live in these crazy times? I've told this story before, but it begs repeating because it makes a valid point here. When I was in college, there was a girlfriend I just couldn't figure out. She was short, stocky, and flat-chested, with thicker-than-average legs. Her hair was a mousy color, and she wore it frizzy and out of control. My girlfriend's face was very average. She just wasn't pretty, certainly not by today's standards of beauty. Despite this, she received loads of attention from the guys. In fact, they swarmed around her! So what was her secret? How did she attract so much attention when she was certainly not beautiful? We went crazy trying to figure this out.

After much watching and observing, I came to a conclusion. The girlfriend had attitude like none I'd ever witnessed before! She believed she was the greatest thing that ever walked the Earth. I'm not kidding when I say she thought a lot of herself. She might have lacked perfection, but she definitely rocked what she had. That girl knew who she was and what she wanted in life, and she went after it in a big way. My girlfriend figured that if a guy didn't play by her rules, he wasn't worth having; if he didn't want her, there must be something wrong with him. Because of this attitude, she could pick and choose just about any man she wanted.

After seeing this firsthand, I can attest to the fact that if you believe you are beautiful, others will also believe you are.

So how can YOU learn to rock what YOU have?

Stop focusing on your negatives.

When you look in a mirror, do you see how beautiful your skin is, how pretty your eyes look with that new sweater, or how long your legs look in your pants? Chances are, you see the flaws staring back at you. "If only I could lose ten pounds...If only my nose was smaller...If only I didn't have this one pimple that looks like a small mountain on my face." For some reason, our brains seem to go right to the negatives without taking notice of the positives. Actually, there's some science to back up why we focus on the flaws instead of the perfection. This just means you need to work even harder to see those things that are definitely working for you. As crazy as it sounds, say them out loud in front of the mirror. This takes practice, but practice makes perfect.

Accept what you can't change.

There are some things I just can't change about myself. No matter how much I want it to happen, I am never going to be taller than five-three. No matter how long I stare in the mirror, my body is never going to look like it did when I was twenty-three. The way I see it, you have two options: You can beat yourself up every time you look in the mirror and be quite dissatisfied with what you see, or you can accept what you've been handed in life and work hard on the things you can control. Personally, I choose the latter; the former eats up way too much of my time and energy. Now, when I look in the mirror and that little voice comments on my changing body and my new wrinkles, I say out loud, "I look great!" I then turn away from the mirror with my sass in place.

If there is something you can't internally accept about your body and you can improve it somehow, just do it!

Let me explain. Let's say you've felt horrible about the size of your breasts your whole life. When people look at you, you feel they only see your less-than-perfect breasts. This has permeated every part of your life and has severely affected your self-esteem. If you know in your heart that your life would be better if you underwent a breast augmentation surgery, then it may be worth it to consider the change. Now, before you over-react to this statement, let me explain it further. I would suggest that you get help from a mental health professional before making such a decision, because there is some risk involved. Once surgery is completed, you might not feel better after all. Some women undergo drastic and permanent changes, only to still feel unsatisfied and move on to another improvement they feel they have to make. See what I'm getting at? Your body is never going to be perfect, and it's fairly easy to find one flaw after another if you are looking hard enough. We all search for what is going to make us happy in life, and for many women, a larger cup size is simply not the answer they are hoping it will be. You should do what makes you feel good about you, but be sure you truly KNOW YOU and what you need to be happy. For this reason, it is wise to seek counsel before scheduling a visit to the cosmetic surgeon.

Make it a habit to move your body.

I don't want to keep saying the same thing over and over, but I have to! Exercise is one of the keys to feeling great about you! It's easy to distinguish a physically active woman from one who isn't: She stands straighter, she has more energy, and she feels good in her own skin. As you get older, it's important to remain active and continue to challenge yourself physically. Do you know how much confidence I received from finishing my forty-five-mile bike-ride? I didn't think I was capable of such a feat, and when I did it, I felt strong, confident, and YOUNG. Honestly, if you don't continue to exercise, you will begin to feel and look old because that's just the way it works. It doesn't matter what age or size you are; if you exercise regularly, you will feel much, much better about your body.

Please girlfriend, will you do me a favor? Be good to your body! It works hard to take you where you need to go in life, and it would appreciate being treated well. Stop being unkind to your body and start treating it with the respect it deserves.

Trust me, girlfriend. You deserve the best, so start living your life like you believe that!

Give it a Little More Thought, Girlfriend

1. Do you waste energy focusing on different aspects of your body? What can you change and what can't you change?

_____

_____

_____

_____

_____

_____

2. What is your plan to change this negative behavior and replace it with something more positive?

_____

_____

_____

_____

_____

_____

Your Call to Action

Make a list of the positive physical attributes you possess. Use adjectives to describe each attribute. For example, maybe you have beautiful, clear skin or sparkling blue eyes. Stand in front of the mirror and state these out loud—as many times as it takes to get you to believe them!

_____

_____

_____

_____

_____

_____

Love Means HAVING to Say You're Sorry

The other day, I was experiencing a loss-of-control moment that involved my son. I hate to admit this, but moments when we lose our self-control happen to the best of us. As my husband likes to say, "People are complicated." My moment happened when I was thinking about the fact that my son needed to find another job. Since he lives ninety miles away and does not call me every minute (which he shouldn't), I can only speculate about what is going on in his life. I believe that to be the reason this even transpired—the speculation on my part. As a few of you probably know, speculation can lead you to jump to ridiculous conclusions. Such is what happened in our morning conversation.

I called my son to ask him how his job search was going. My communication delivery was negatively affected by all the time I had spent worrying. He tersely replied that he couldn't talk because he was at work and had to go. When he got off work, he gave me a call and articulated, "Mom, you do not know everything going on in my life. I am an adult. This is my responsibility, and it was very inappropriate for you to call me at work to have that conversation." Busted! He was much more mature about the situation than I had been, and I was as embarrassed as I was impressed. I realized I had raised a smart, articulate, wise young man.

Feeling ridiculous, I apologized to him and told him he had every right to be angry with me. I was out of line asking him questions and interrupting him at work. Did it feel good apologizing to him? No! It felt horrible admitting my behavior was abhorrent, but it also felt very right. He accepted my apology and said he understood that my words came from a good place. But what would have happened to our relationship if the apology hadn't been given and accepted?

I know women who have difficulty apologizing and accepting apologies. I understand why it's difficult, and I admit it is hard for me as well. The point is that it's hard for all of us to admit it when we've been wrong. It just doesn't feel good to say you messed up. You must be cognizant of the fact that if you want a good relationship with the people you care about, the apology has to happen. If you want to feel good about you, you need to be able to say you are sorry when an apology is warranted. The bottom line is this: If you want to have character and sass, you need to be able to say you are sorry and move on.

Do you have difficulty accepting apologies? Are you one of those women who simmers and stews for days, weeks, years, or forever? You might believe, deep down, that not accepting an apology forces the other individual to suffer. This might be an enjoyable, vengeful feeling if they've hurt you in some way. The truth is, you couldn't be more wrong!

Think back to your childhood and your relationship with your parents. Do you remember instances when your mother or father had difficulty saying they were sorry? Did either one of them hold grudges and refuse to speak with someone if they were angry? If you remember any of this behavior, you need to realize that this was your training ground for how to handle conflict and apologies. You learned how to handle disagreements and how to resolve situations by the patterns set in your home. Your behavior today is greatly affected by the model that was present in your own family unit.

The person who truly suffers when you don't accept an apology is YOU. Eventually, you will realize that refusing to accept an apology weighs you down and becomes your baggage in life. This can manifest in your behavior in a variety of ways, simmering just beneath the surface and restricting you from fully enjoying your life.

So, my advice is to let go of whatever you're holding on to that is weighing you down. When you're ready and in the right place, just forgive. In the end, it doesn't matter if you feel you are right or wrong. Do this for your own mental health and your sanity. You have nothing to lose and *everything* to gain.

A Word to the Wise

It is important for me to add a word to the wise at this time. If someone has hurt you deeply time and time again, do not go back for more! Accept the apology and develop some boundaries in your life to protect yourself from that person, even if it is a family member. Remember that respect is a two-way street. Accepting an apology does not mean opening yourself up to repeated hurts. Allow yourself to accept the apology so you can get on with life and be happy. So let go, keep your **firm boundaries,** and get on with your life, girlfriend!

Being able to give and accept an apology is an essential part of living a healthy emotional life.

Give it a Little More Thought, Girlfriend

1. Do you have any trouble saying you're sorry? If so, how has this affected your relationships?

_____

_____

_____

_____

_____

_____

2. Did your parents have difficulty giving or receiving an apology? How did this affect you?

_____

_____

_____

_____

_____

_____

3. Do you struggle with accepting apologies? How does this make you feel?

_____

_____

_____

_____

_____

_____

Your Call to Action

Describe a time when you had difficulty accepting or receiving an apology. Write down some of the feelings and emotions you experienced during this time and why it was so difficult to move forward.

_____

_____

_____

_____

_____

_____

One to Grow On: I've Got the Power!

Choices: Some women don't feel like they have any in life. Do you know how many times I've heard that? Almost every client I work with alludes to this at some point in the beginning of our work. Time after time, I'll hear the comment thrown around by a girlfriend who's struggling to find happiness. You know what? It drives me crazy! Just by saying that we don't have any choices, we've made our decision to stay miserable and unhappy. We have made our choice! We have usurped our power as women. But why do we all insist on doing this at some point in our life?

You get comfortable being unhappy.

Yes, girlfriend, at some point, you become very comfortable being unhappy—way too comfortable. You get stuck in unhappiness like a gerbil spinning his wheel, unable to get off. It becomes your way of life. Being unhappy becomes a way to live daily, and you can't imagine any other way. Sometimes it's difficult to see any other way because of the many negative conversations you've had in your head. It becomes your "norm," and before you know it, days, weeks, and months pass while you ignore the fact that only you have the power to change your situation.

You get scared of what's on the other side.

It is so easy to say, "I have no choice." When you say this, you don't have to worry or ask "What if I make this choice and am still unhappy? What will I do then? What will it look like?" That can terrify us enough to stay exactly where we are. Yes, it is scary when you don't know what's going to happen and you get outside your comfort zone, but it's also thrilling...and it's truly what life is about.

You don't believe in you.

Yes, girlfriend, that's really what it comes down to:

believing in you. If you believe, you will find a way to make it work out. So here's the truth: Believing you work out. So here's the truth: Believing you have choices in life and taking that step is a way for you to get to the believing-in-you part. Once you see that you *do* have the power, strength, and courage to change, you have a choice. When you make a choice, **then** you begin to believe in *you*. Really, it's one of those which-came-first-the-chicken-or-the-egg? things.

It lets you off the hook.

Convincing yourself that you have no choices or power to change your situation lets you off the hook in life. It enables you to take absolutely no responsibility for where you are in the world. If you allow yourself to think this way, you can continue to blame others for your own unhappiness. Maybe it's your boss, cheating husband, or verbally abusive mom's fault that you are continuing down your current path. It's never YOUR fault. Way to take away every last ounce of your own power, girlfriend! When you actually take responsibility, that changes everything. Then, you need to do some hard work, and that can be difficult and scary. There isn't a woman on the planet who hasn't fallen victim to this behavioral pattern. The sad part is that some women engage in this behavior over and over throughout their lifetime. They never learn from their past experiences and move ahead in life. They insist on being **powerless** in life, always feeling they have no choice but to continue to live their miserable existence.

So, here you are, girlfriend. You have finished the 31 days to finding your sass, and you are now in on the principles that will guide you to living a healthy, happy, successful life. There is only one thing missing now...

Acknowledge your POWER and use it to live your dream life!!

You have the power to achieve your dreams. All you need to do is BELIEVE in YOU!

Give it a Little More Thought, Girlfriend

1. Has there ever been a time in your life when you felt you had no choice but to continue down the same old path?

_____

_____

_____

_____

2. What do you think was your reason for getting stuck?

_____

_____

_____

_____

Your Call to Action

Describe a time in your life when you were truly able to feel your power as a woman. Write down some of the feelings and emotions you experienced during that time.

_____

_____

_____

_____

_____

_____